TEACHER'S DAY

teachersday

11월 수능 날 '1시 10분'
그 날의 '1시간 10분'이 여러분의 날이 될 것이다.

STUDENT'S DAY

고1: 4단계 (변형문제)

22년 9월 전국연합학력평가

스승의날 수능·내신대비교재

모의고사 「1시 10분」

스승의날
Teachers Day Publisher

contents

목 차

어법 선택 (A)

2022년_고1_9월_인천광역시 교육청_학력평가_18번

1. 다음 글의 괄호 안에서 어법에 맞는 표현을 고르시오.

Dear Parents/Guardians, Class parties will 1)[hold / be held] on the afternoon December 16th, 2022. Children may bring in sweets, crisps, biscuits, cakes, and drinks. We are 2)[requesting / requested] that children do not bring in home-cooked or prepared food. All food should arrive in a sealed packet with the ingredients 3)[clear / clearly] 4)[listed / listing / list]. Fruit and vegetables are welcomed 5)[whether / if] they are pre-packed in a sealed packet from the shop. Please DO NOT send any food into school 6)[containing / contained] nuts 7)[due to / as] we have many children with severe nut allergies. Please check the ingredients of all food your children bring 8)[careful / carefully]. Thank you for your continued support and cooperation.
Yours sincerely, Lisa Brown, Headteacher

2022년_고1_9월_인천광역시 교육청_학력평가_19번

2. 다음 글의 괄호 안에서 어법에 맞는 표현을 고르시오.

It was two hours before the submission deadline and I still 9)[haven't / hadn't / didn't] finished my news article. I sat at the desk, but suddenly, the typewriter didn't work. No matter how 10)[I tapped hard / hard I tapped] the keys, the levers wouldn't move to strike the paper. I started to realize 11)[which / what / that] I would not be able to finish the article on time. Desperately, I rested the typewriter on my lap and started hitting each key with as much force as I could 12)[manage / be managed]. Nothing happened. Thinking something might 13)[happen / have happened] inside of it, I opened the cover, lifted up the keys, and found the problem — a paper clip. The keys had no room to move. After 14)[picking / picked] it out, I pressed and pulled some parts. The keys moved 15)[smooth / smoothly] again. I breathed deeply and smiled. Now I knew that I could finish my article on time.

2022년_고1_9월_인천광역시 교육청_학력평가_20번

3. 다음 글의 괄호 안에서 어법에 맞는 표현을 고르시오.

Experts on writing say, "Get rid of as many words as 16)[possible / possibly].." Each 17)[word / words] must do 18)[important something / something important]. If it doesn't, get rid of it. Well, this doesn't work for speaking. It takes more words to introduce, express, and adequately 19)[elaborate / elaborates] an idea in speech than it takes in writing. Why is this so? 20)[During / While] the reader can reread, the listener cannot rehear. Speakers do not come 21)[equipping / equipped / equip] with a replay button. Because listeners are easily 22)[distracting / distracted], they will miss many pieces of 23)[what / which / that] a speaker says. If they miss the crucial sentence, they may never catch up. This makes 24)[it / them] necessary for speakers to talk longer about their points, 25)[use / using / used] more words on them than would be 26)[using / used] to express the same idea in writing.

2022년_고1_9월_인천광역시 교육청_학력평가_21번

4. 다음 글의 괄호 안에서 어법에 맞는 표현을 고르시오.

Is the customer always right? When customers return a broken product to a famous company, 27)[which / that / what] makes kitchen and bathroom fixtures, the company nearly always offers a replacement to maintain good customer relations. Still, "there are times you've got to say 'no,'" explains the warranty expert of the company, such as when a product is undamaged or has 28)[abused / been abused]. Entrepreneur Lauren Thorp, who owns an e-commerce company, says, "While the customer is 'always' right, sometimes you just have to fire a customer." When Thorp has 29)[tried / been tried] everything 30)[resolving / to resolve] a complaint and realizes 31)[which / what / that] the customer will be 32)[dissatisfying / dissatisfied] no matter what, she returns her attention to the rest of her customers, who she says 33)[is / are / do / does] "the reason for my success."

2022년_고1_9월_인천광역시 교육청_학력평가_22번

5. 다음 글의 괄호 안에서 어법에 맞는 표현을 고르시오.

A recent study from Carnegie Mellon University in Pittsburgh, called "When Too Much of a Good Thing May Be Bad," indicates that classrooms with too much decoration 34)[be / is / are] a source of distraction for young children and directly affect their cognitive performance. Being visually 35)[overstimulating / overstimulated], the children have a great deal of difficulty 36)[concentrating / concentrated / concentrate] and end up with worse academic results. On the other hand, if there is not much decoration on the classroom walls, the children are less 37)[distracting / distracted], spend more time on their activities, and learn more. So it's our job, in order to 38)[support / supporting] their attention, to find the right balance between excessive decoration and the complete absence of it.

2022년_고1_9월_인천광역시 교육청_학력평가_23번

6. 다음 글의 괄호 안에서 어법에 맞는 표현을 고르시오.

For creatures like us, evolution smiled upon those with a strong 39)[need / needed / needing] to belong. Survival and reproduction 40)[is / are] the criteria of success by natural selection, and 41)[forming / formed] relationships with other people can be useful for both survival and reproduction. Groups can share resources, care for sick members, scare off predators, fight together against enemies, divide tasks so as 42)[for / to] improve efficiency, and contribute to survival in many other ways. In particular, if an individual and a group 43)[want / wants] the same resource, the group will generally prevail, so competition for resources would especially favor a need to belong. Belongingness will likewise promote reproduction, such as by bringing potential mates into contact with each other, and in particular by keeping parents together to care for their children, who are much more likely to 44)[survive / surviving] if they have more than one caregiver.

2022년_고1_9월_인천광역시 교육청_학력평가_24번

7. 다음 글의 괄호 안에서 어법에 맞는 표현을 고르시오.

Many people make a mistake of only operating along the safe zones, and in the process they miss the opportunity to achieve greater things. They 45)[are / do] so 46)[because / because of] a fear of the unknown and a fear of treading the unknown paths of life. Those that are 47)[brave enough / enough brave] to take those roads less 48)[travelling / travelled] 49)[be / is / are] able to get great returns and 50)[derive / derive from] major satisfaction out of their courageous moves. Being overcautious will mean that you will miss 51)[attaining / to attain] the greatest levels of your potential. You must learn to take those chances 52)[that / what] many people around you will not take, because your success will flow from those bold decisions that you will take along the way.

*tread: 밟다

2022년_고1_9월_인천광역시 교육청_학력평가_25번

8. 다음 글의 괄호 안에서 어법에 맞는 표현을 고르시오.

The graph above shows the share of the urban population by continent in 1950 and in 2020. For each continent, the share of the urban population in 2020 was larger than 53)[it / those / that] in 1950. From 1950 to 2020, the share of the urban population in Africa increased from 14.3% to 43.5%. The share of the urban population in Asia was the second lowest in 1950 but not in 2020. In 1950, the share of the urban population in Europe was larger than 54)[that / those] in Latin America and the Caribbean, whereas the reverse was true in 2020. Among the five continents, Northern America was 55)[ranking / ranked] in the first position for the share of the urban population in both 1950 and 2020.

9. 다음 글의 괄호 안에서 어법에 맞는 표현을 고르시오.

Wilbur Smith was a South African novelist specialising in historical fiction. Smith wanted to become a journalist, 56)[**writing / wrote / written**] about social conditions in South Africa, but his father was never supportive of his writing and forced him 57)[**getting / to get**] a real job. Smith studied further and became a tax accountant, but he finally turned back to his love of writing. He wrote his first novel, The Gods First Make Mad, and 58)[**was / has / had**] received 20 rejections by 1962. In 1964, Smith published another novel, When the Lion Feeds, and it went on to 59)[**be / being**] successful, 60)[**selling / sold**] around the world. A famous actor and film producer bought the film rights for When the Lion Feeds, 61)[**despite of / in spite of / despite / although**] no movie resulted. By the time of his death in 2021 he had 62)[**published / been published**] 49 novels, selling more than 140 million copies worldwide.

10. 다음 글의 괄호 안에서 어법에 맞는 표현을 고르시오.

2022 Springfield Park Yoga Class
The popular yoga class in Springfield Park returns! Enjoy yoga 63)[**hosted / hosted on**] the park lawn. 64)[**If / Unless**] you can't make it to the park, join us online on our social media platforms!
◆When: Saturdays, 2 p.m. to 3 p.m., September
◆Registration: At least TWO hours before each class 65)[**starts / will start**], sign up here.
◆Notes
•For online classes: find a quiet space with enough room 66)[**for / of**] you to stretch out.
•For classes in the park: mats are not 67)[**providing / provided**], so bring your own!
※The class will be 68)[**canceled / canceling**] if the weather is unfavorable. For more information, click here.

11. 다음 글의 괄호 안에서 어법에 맞는 표현을 고르시오.

Kenner High School's Water Challenge
Kenner High School's Water Challenge is a new contest to propose measures against water pollution. Please share your ideas for dealing with water pollution!
Submission
How: Submit your proposal by email to admin@khswater.edu.
When: September 5, 2022 to September 23, 2022
Details: Participants must enter in teams of four and can only 69)[**join / join with**] one team.
Submission is 70)[**limiting / limited**] to one proposal per 71)[**team / teams**].
Participants must use the proposal form 72)[**providing / provide / provided**] on the website.
Prizes
1st: $50 gift certificate
2nd: $30 gift certificate
3rd: $10 gift certificate
Please visit www.khswater.edu to learn more about the challenge.

12. 다음 글의 괄호 안에서 어법에 맞는 표현을 고르시오.

The human brain, it turns out, has 73)[**shrunk / been shrunk**] in mass by about 10 percent since it peaked in size 15,000-30,000 years ago. One possible reason is that many thousands of years ago humans lived in a world of dangerous predators where they had to have their wits about them at all times to avoid 74)[**to be / being**] killed. Today, we have effectively domesticated ourselves and many of the tasks of survival — from avoiding immediate death to building shelters to 75)[**obtain / obtaining**] food — have been outsourced to the wider society. We are smaller than our ancestors too, and it is a characteristic of domestic animals that they are generally smaller than their wild cousins. None of this may mean we are dumber — brain size is not necessarily an indicator of human intelligence — but it may mean 76)[**that / which / what**] our brains today are 77)[**wiring / wired**] up differently, and perhaps more efficiently, than those of our ancestors.

13. 다음 글의 괄호 안에서 어법에 맞는 표현을 고르시오.

It is widely believed that certain herbs somehow magically improve the work of certain organs, and "cure" specific diseases as a result. Such statements are unscientific and groundless. Sometimes herbs 78)[**appear / are appeared**] to work, 79)[**due to / because of / since**] they tend to increase your blood circulation in an aggressive attempt by your body to eliminate them from your system. That can create a temporary feeling of a high, 80)[**what / that / which**] makes it seem as if your health condition has improved. Also, herbs can have a placebo effect, just like any other method, thus 81)[**helping / helped**] you feel better. Whatever the case, it is your body 82)[**that / which / what**] 83)[**have / has**] the intelligence to regain health, and not the herbs. How can herbs have the intelligence needed to direct your body into getting healthier? That is impossible. Try to imagine how herbs might 84)[**come / be come**] into your body and intelligently fix your problems. If you try to do that, you will see how 85)[**it seems impossible / impossible it seems**]. Otherwise, it would mean that herbs are more intelligent than the human body, 86)[**which / what / that**] is truly hard to 87)[**believe / believing**].

*placebo effect: 위약 효과

14. 다음 글의 괄호 안에서 어법에 맞는 표현을 고르시오.

We worry that the robots are 88)[**taking / taken**] our jobs, but just as common a problem is that the robots are taking our judgment. In the large warehouses so common behind the scenes of today's economy, human 'pickers' hurry around grabbing products off shelves and moving them to where they can be packed and 89)[**dispatch / dispatched**]. In their ears are headpieces: the voice of 'Jennifer', a piece of software, 90)[**tell / tells / telling**] them where to go and what to do, 91)[**controls / controlled / controlling**] the smallest details of their movements. Jennifer breaks down instructions into tiny chunks, to minimise error and maximise productivity — for example, rather than picking eighteen copies of a book off a shelf, the human worker would be politely 92)[**instructing / instructed**] to pick five. Then another five. Then yet another five. Then another three. Working in such conditions 93)[**reduce / reduces**] people to machines made of flesh. Rather than asking us to think or adapt, the Jennifer unit takes over the thought process and treats workers as an inexpensive source of some visual processing and a pair of opposable thumbs.

*dispatch: 발송하다 **chunk: 덩어리

2022년_고1_9월_인천광역시 교육청_학력평가_32번

15. 다음 글의 괄호 안에서 어법에 맞는 표현을 고르시오.

The 94)[**prevailing** / **prevailed**] view among developmental scientists 95)[**is** / **are**] that people are active contributors to their own development. People are influenced by the physical and social contexts 96)[**which** / **what** / **in which**] they live, but they also play a role in influencing their development by interacting with, and changing, those contexts. Even infants influence the world around them and construct their own development through their interactions. Consider an infant who smiles at each 97)[**adult** / **adults**] he sees; he influences his world 98)[**due to** / **because**] adults are likely to 99)[**smile** / **smiling**], use "baby talk," and play with him in response. The infant brings adults into close contact, making one-on-one interactions and 100)[**creates** / **created** / **creating**] opportunities for learning. By engaging the world around them, thinking, being curious, and 101)[**interact** / **interacted** / **interacting**] with people, objects, and the world around them, individuals of all ages are "manufacturers of their own development."

2022년_고1_9월_인천광역시 교육청_학력평가_33번

16. 다음 글의 괄호 안에서 어법에 맞는 표현을 고르시오.

The demand for freshness can have 102)[**hiding** / **hidden**] environmental costs. While freshness is now 103)[**using** / **being used**] as a term in food marketing as part of a return to nature, the demand for year-round supplies of fresh produce such as soft fruit and exotic vegetables 104)[**have** / **has**] led to the widespread use of hot houses in cold climates and increasing reliance on total quality control — management by temperature control, use of pesticides and computer /satellite-based logistics. The demand for freshness has also 105)[**contributed** / **been contributed**] to concerns about food wastage. Use of 'best before', 'sell by' and 'eat by' labels 106)[**have** / **has**] legally allowed institutional waste. Campaigners have 107)[**exposed** / **been exposed**] the scandal of overproduction and waste. Tristram Stuart, one of the global band of anti-waste 108)[**campaigner** / **campaigners**], argues that, with 109)[**fresh** / **freshly**] 110)[**making** / **made**] sandwiches, over-ordering is standard practice across the retail sector to avoid the appearance of empty shelf space, 111)[**leading** / **led** / **leads**] to high volumes of waste when supply regularly exceeds demand.

* pesticide: 살충제 ** logistics: 물류, 유통

2022년_고1_9월_인천광역시 교육청_학력평가_34번

17. 다음 글의 괄호 안에서 어법에 맞는 표현을 고르시오.

In the studies of Colin Cherry at the Massachusetts Institute for Technology back in the 1950s, his participants listened to voices in one ear at a time and then through both ears in an effort to determine 112)[what / whether] we can listen to two people 113)[talk / talked / to talk] at the same time. One ear always 114)[contained / contained with] a message that the listener had to repeat back (called "shadowing") while the other ear 115)[included with / included] people speaking. The trick was to 116)[see / seeing] if you could totally focus on the main message and also hear someone talking in your other ear. Cleverly, Cherry found 117)[it / them] was impossible 118)[for / of] his participants to know whether the message in the other ear was 119)[speaking / spoken] by a man or woman, in English or another language, or 120)[was / were] even comprised of real words at all! In other words, people could not process two pieces of information at the same time.

2022년_고1_9월_인천광역시 교육청_학력평가_35번

18. 다음 글의 괄호 안에서 어법에 맞는 표현을 고르시오.

The fast-paced evolution of Information and Communication Technologies (ICTs) has radically 121)[transformed / been transformed] the dynamics and business models of the tourism and hospitality industry. This leads to new levels/forms of competitiveness among service providers and transforms the customer experience through new services. Creating unique experiences and providing convenient services to customers 122)[lead / leads] to satisfaction and, eventually, customer loyalty to the service provider or brand (i.e., hotels). In particular, the most recent technological boost 123)[receiving / received] by the tourism sector 124)[is / are] 125)[representing / represented] by mobile applications. Indeed, 126)[empowering / being empowered] tourists with mobile access to services such as hotel reservations, airline ticketing, and recommendations for local attractions 127)[generating / generate / generates] strong interest and considerable profits.

* hospitality industry: 서비스업(호텔·식당업 등)

2022년_고1_9월_인천광역시 교육청_학력평가_36번

19. 다음 글의 괄호 안에서 어법에 맞는 표현을 고르시오.

With nearly a billion hungry people in the world, there is obviously no single cause. However, far and away the biggest cause is poverty. Seventy-nine percent of the world's hungry 128)[live / lives] in nations 129)[that / what] are net exporters of food. How can this be? The reason people are hungry in those countries 130)[is / are] that the products 131)[producing / produced] there can be sold on the world market for more than the local citizens can afford to 132)[pay / paying] for them. In the modern age you do not starve 133)[because of / because] you have no food, you starve because you have no money. So the problem really is 134)[which / what / that] food is, in the grand scheme of things, too expensive and many people are 135)[so / very / too] poor 136)[buying / to buy] it. The answer will be in continuing the trend of lowering the cost of food.

* net exporter: 순 수출국 ** scheme: 체계, 조직

2022년_고1_9월_인천광역시 교육청_학력평가_37번

20. 다음 글의 괄호 안에서 어법에 맞는 표현을 고르시오.

Most people have a perfect time of day when they feel they 137)[are / being] at their best, whether in the morning, evening, or afternoon. Some of us are night owls, some early birds, and others in between may feel most 138)[active / actively] during the afternoon hours. If you are able to organize your day and divide your work, make it a point to deal with tasks 139)[that / what] demand attention at your best time of the day. However, if the task you face 140)[demanding / demand / demands] creativity and novel ideas, it's best to tackle it at your "worst" time of day! So if you are an early bird, make sure 141)[attacking / to attack] your creative task in the evening, and vice versa for night owls. When your mind and body are less alert than at your "peak" hours, the muse of creativity awakens and is 142)[allowing / allowed] to roam more 143)[free / freely]. In other words, when your mental machinery is loose rather than standing at attention, the creativity 144)[flows / is flowed].

*roam: (어슬렁어슬렁) 거닐다

2022년_고1_9월_인천광역시 교육청_학력평가_38번

21. 다음 글의 괄호 안에서 어법에 맞는 표현을 고르시오.

Television is the number one leisure activity in the United States and Europe, 145)[**consumes / consumed / consuming**] more than half of our free time. We generally think of television as a way to relax, tune out, and escape from our troubles for a bit each day. 146)[**During / While**] this is true, there is increasing evidence that we are more 147)[**motivating / motivated**] to tune in to our favorite shows and characters when we are feeling lonely or have a greater need for social connection. Television watching does 148)[**satisfy / satisfies / satisfying**] these social needs to some extent, at least in the short run. Unfortunately, it is also likely to "crowd out" other activities 149)[**that / what / in which**] produce more sustainable social contributions to our social well-being. The 150)[**more / most / many**] television we watch, the less likely we are to volunteer our time or 151)[**spending / to spend**] time with people in our social networks. In other words, 152)[**a / the**] more time we make for Friends, 153)[**a / the**] less time we have for friends in real life.

　　*Friends: 프렌즈(미국의 한 방송국에서 방영된 시트콤)

2022년_고1_9월_인천광역시 교육청_학력평가_39번

22. 다음 글의 괄호 안에서 어법에 맞는 표현을 고르시오.

We often associate the concept of temperature with how hot or cold 154)[**feels an object / an object feels**] when we touch it. In this way, our senses provide us with a qualitative indication of temperature. Our senses, however, are unreliable and often mislead us. For example, if you stand in bare feet with one foot on carpet and the other on a tile floor, the tile feels colder than the carpet 155)[**despite / despite of / even though**] both 156)[**is / are**] at the same temperature. The two objects feel 157)[**different / differently**] 158)[**because of / because**] tile transfers energy by heat at a higher rate than carpet 159)[**does / is**]. Your skin "measures" the rate of energy transfer by heat rather than the actual temperature. 160)[**That / Which / What**] we need is a reliable and reproducible method for measuring the relative hotness or coldness of objects rather than the rate of energy transfer. Scientists have 161)[**developed / been developed**] a variety of thermometers for making such quantitative measurements.

　　*thermometer: 온도계

2022년_고1_9월_인천광역시 교육청_학력평가_40번

23. 다음 글의 괄호 안에서 어법에 맞는 표현을 고르시오.

My colleagues and I ran an experiment testing two different messages 162)[**meaning / meant**] to convince thousands of resistant alumni 163)[**making / to make**] a donation. One message emphasized the opportunity to do good: donating would benefit students, faculty, and staff. The other emphasized the opportunity to feel good: donors would enjoy the warm glow of giving. The two messages were equally effective: in both cases, 6.5 percent of the unwilling alumni ended up 164)[**donate / donated / donating**]. Then we combined them, 165)[**beacuse of / because**] two reasons are better than one. Except they 166)[**didn't / weren't**]. When we put the two reasons together, the 167)[**given / giving**] rate dropped below 3 percent. Each reason alone was more than twice as 168)[**effective / effectively**] as the two combined. The audience was already skeptical. When we gave them different kinds of reasons to donate, we triggered their awareness 169)[**that / which / what**] someone was trying to persuade them — and they shielded 170)[**them / themselves**] against it.

　　* alumni: 졸업생 ** skeptical: 회의적인

⬇

In the experiment mentioned above, when the two different reasons to donate were 171)[**giving / given**] simultaneously, the audience was less likely to be 172)[**convinced / convincing**] because they could recognize the intention to persuade them.

2022년_고1_9월_인천광역시 교육청_학력평가_41~42번

24. 다음 글의 괄호 안에서 어법에 맞는 표현을 고르시오.

In a society that rejects the consumption of insects there are some individuals who overcome this rejection, but most will continue with this attitude. 173)[That / It] may be very difficult to convince an entire society 174)[what / which / that] insects are totally suitable for consumption. However, there are examples 175)[which / in which] this reversal of attitudes about certain foods 176)[have / has / had] happened to an entire society. Several examples in the past 120 years from European-American society 177)[being / is / are]: considering lobster a luxury food instead of a food for servants and prisoners; considering sushi a safe and delicious food; and considering pizza not just a food for the rural poor of Sicily. In Latin American countries, 178)[which / what / where] insects are already 179)[consuming / consumed], a portion of the population hates their consumption and 180)[associate / associates] it with poverty. There are also examples of people who have had the habit of consuming them and abandoned that habit 181)[because / due to] shame, and because they do not want to 182)[categorize / be categorized] as 183)[poor / poorly] or uncivilized. According to Esther Katz, an anthropologist, if the consumption of insects as a food luxury 184)[is / are] to be 185)[promoting / promoted], there would be more chances that some individuals who do not present this habit 186)[overcoming / overcome] ideas 187)[which / under which] they were 188)[educating / educated]. And this could also help to revalue the consumption of insects by those people who already eat them.

어휘 선택 (A)

2022년_고1_9월_인천광역시 교육청_학력평가_20번

1. 다음 글의 괄호 안에서 문맥에 맞는 어휘를 고르시오.

Experts on writing say, "Get rid of as many words as possible." Each word must do something 189)[trivial / significant]. If it doesn't, 190)[reserve / eliminate] it. Well, this doesn't work for speaking. It takes more words to introduce, express, and adequately elaborate an idea in speech than it takes in writing. Why is this so? While the reader can reread, the listener cannot rehear. Speakers do not come furnished with a replay button. Because listeners are easily 191)[focused / diverted], they will 192)[catch / overlook] many pieces of what a speaker says. If they miss the crucial sentence, they may never catch up. This makes it 193)[secondary / vital] for speakers to talk longer about their points, using more words on them than would be used to express the same idea in writing.

2022년_고1_9월_인천광역시 교육청_학력평가_21번

2. 다음 글의 괄호 안에서 문맥에 맞는 어휘를 고르시오.

Is the customer always right? When customers return a broken product to a famous company, which makes kitchen and bathroom fixtures, the company nearly always 194)[cancels / provides] a replacement to maintain good customer relations. Still, "there are times you've got to say 'no,'" explains the warranty expert of the company, such as when a product is 195)[impaired / intact] or has been abused. Entrepreneur Lauren Thorp, who owns an e-commerce company, says, "While the customer is 'always' right, sometimes you just have to 196)[employ / lay off] a customer." When Thorp has tried everything to resolve a complaint and realizes that the customer will be 197)[contented / discontented] no matter what, she returns her attention to the rest of her customers, who she says are "the reason for my success."

2022년_고1_9월_인천광역시 교육청_학력평가_22번

3. 다음 글의 괄호 안에서 문맥에 맞는 어휘를 고르시오.

A recent study from Carnegie Mellon University in Pittsburgh, called "When Too Much of a Good Thing May Be Bad," indicates that classrooms with too much decoration are a source of 198)[composure / confusion] for young children and directly affect their cognitive performance. Being visually overstimulated, the children have a great deal of difficulty concentrating and end up with 199)[better / worse] academic results. On the other hand, if there is not much decoration on the classroom walls, the children are 200)[more / less] distracted, spend 201)[less / more] time on their activities, and learn more. So it's our job, in order to support their attention, to find the right balance between 202)[superfluous / adequate] decoration and the complete absence of it.

2022년_고1_9월_인천광역시 교육청_학력평가_23번

4. 다음 글의 괄호 안에서 문맥에 맞는 어휘를 고르시오.

For creatures like us, evolution smiled upon those with a 203)[scarce / intense] need to belong. Survival and reproduction are the criteria of success by natural selection, and forming relationships with other people can be 204)[disadvantageous / advantageous] for both survival and reproduction. Groups can share resources, care for sick members, scare off predators, fight together against enemies, divide tasks so as to improve efficiency, and contribute to survival in many other ways. In particular, if an individual and a group want the same resource, the group will generally prevail, so competition for resources would especially 205)[impair / benefit] a need to belong. Belongingness will likewise 206)[inhibit / foster] reproduction, such as by bringing potential mates into contact with each other, and in particular by keeping parents together to care for their children, who are much more likely to survive if they have 207)[sole / multiple] caregiver(s).

스승의날 영어연구소

2022년_고1_9월_인천광역시 교육청_학력평가_24번

5. 다음 글의 괄호 안에서 문맥에 맞는 어휘를 고르시오.

Many people make a mistake of only operating along the safe zones, and in the process they 208)[**grab / lose**] the opportunity to achieve greater things. They do so because of a fear of the unknown and a fear of treading the unknown paths of life. Those that are brave enough to take those roads 209)[**more / less**] travelled are 210)[**unable / able**] to get great returns and 211)[**deprive / derive**] major satisfaction out of their 212)[**cowardly / bold**] moves. Being too 213)[**careless / discreet**] will mean that you will miss attaining the greatest levels of your potential. You must learn to take those chances that many people around you will not take, because your success will flow from those bold decisions that you will take along the way.

2022년_고1_9월_인천광역시 교육청_학력평가_26번

6. 다음 글의 괄호 안에서 문맥에 맞는 어휘를 고르시오.

Wilbur Smith was a South African novelist specialising in historical fiction. Smith wanted to become a journalist, writing about social conditions in South Africa, but his father never 214)[**discouraged / encouraged**] his writing and forced him to get a real job. Smith studied further and became a tax accountant, but he finally turned back to his love of writing. He wrote his first novel, The Gods First Make Mad, and had received 20 215)[**permits / rejections**] by 1962. In 1964, Smith published another novel, When the Lion Feeds, and it went on to be successful, selling around the world. A famous actor and film producer bought the film rights for When the Lion Feeds, although no movie resulted. By the time of his death in 2021 he had published 49 novels, selling more than 140 million copies worldwide.

2022년_고1_9월_인천광역시 교육청_학력평가_29번

7. 다음 글의 괄호 안에서 문맥에 맞는 어휘를 고르시오.

The human brain, it turns out, has 216)[**expanded / contracted**] in mass by about 10 percent since it peaked in size 15,000-30,000 years ago. One possible reason is that many thousands of years ago humans lived in a world of 217)[**mild / fierce**] predators where they had to have their wits about them at all times to avoid being killed. Today, we have effectively domesticated ourselves and many of the tasks of survival — from avoiding immediate death to building shelters to obtaining food — have been outsourced to the wider society. We are 218)[**bigger / smaller**] than our ancestors too, and it is a characteristic of domestic animals that they are generally 219)[**bigger / smaller**] than their wild cousins. None of this may mean we are 220)[**intelligent / unintelligent**] — brain size is not necessarily an indicator of human intelligence — but it may mean that our brains today are wired up differently, and perhaps more efficiently, than those of our ancestors.

2022년_고1_9월_인천광역시 교육청_학력평가_30번

8. 다음 글의 괄호 안에서 문맥에 맞는 어휘를 고르시오.

It is widely believed that certain herbs somehow magically 221)[**weaken / enhance**] the work of certain organs, and "cure" specific diseases as a result. Such statements are unscientific and 222)[**logical / illogical**]. Sometimes herbs appear to work, since they tend to 223)[**diminish / boost**] your blood circulation in an aggressive attempt by your body to eliminate them from your system. That can create a 224)[**permanent / momentary**] feeling of a high, which makes it seem as if your health condition has 225)[**undermined / enhanced**]. Also, herbs can have a placebo effect, just like any other method, thus helping you feel better. Whatever the case, it is your body that has the intelligence to regain health, and not the herbs. How can herbs have the intelligence needed to direct your body into getting healthier? That is 226)[**possible / implausible**]. Try to imagine how herbs might come into your body and intelligently fix your problems. If you try to do that, you will see how impossible it seems. Otherwise, it would mean that herbs are 227)[**less / more**] intelligent than the human body, which is truly 228)[**hard / easy**] to believe.

*placebo effect: 위약 효과

2022년_고1_9월_인천광역시 교육청_학력평가_31번

9. 다음 글의 괄호 안에서 문맥에 맞는 어휘를 고르시오.

We worry that the robots are taking our jobs, but just as 229)[rare / usual] a problem is that the robots are taking our judgment. In the large warehouses so common behind the scenes of today's economy, human 'pickers' hurry around grabbing products off shelves and moving them to where they can be packed and dispatched. In their ears are headpieces: the voice of 'Jennifer', a piece of software, tells them where to go and what to do, controlling the smallest details of their movements. Jennifer breaks down instructions into tiny chunks, to minimise error and maximise productivity — for example, rather than picking eighteen copies of a book off a shelf, the human worker would be politely instructed to pick five. Then another five. Then yet another five. Then another three. Working in such conditions 230)[extends / confines] people to machines made of flesh. Rather than asking us to think or adapt, the Jennifer unit takes over the thought process and treats workers as a 231)[costly / cheap] source of some visual processing and a pair of opposable thumbs.

*dispatch: 발송하다 **chunk: 덩어리

2022년_고1_9월_인천광역시 교육청_학력평가_32번

10. 다음 글의 괄호 안에서 문맥에 맞는 어휘를 고르시오.

The prevailing view among developmental scientists is that people are 232)[passive / aggressive] contributors to their own development. People are influenced by the physical and social contexts in which they live, but they also play a role in influencing their development by interacting with, and 233)[maintaining / modifying], those contexts. Even infants influence the world around them and construct their own development through their interactions. Consider an infant who smiles at each adult he sees; he influences his world because adults are 234)[unlikely / likely] to smile, use "baby talk," and play with him in response. The infant brings adults into close contact, making one-on-one interactions and creating opportunities for learning. By engaging the world around them, thinking, being curious, and interacting with people, objects, and the world around them, individuals of all ages are "manufacturers of their own development."

2022년_고1_9월_인천광역시 교육청_학력평가_33번

11. 다음 글의 괄호 안에서 문맥에 맞는 어휘를 고르시오.

The demand for 235)[familiarity / novelty] can have hidden environmental costs. While freshness is now being used as a term in food marketing as part of a return to nature, the demand for year-round supplies of fresh produce such as soft fruit and exotic vegetables has led to the 236)[specific / extensive] use of hot houses in cold climates and 237)[decreasing / increasing] reliance on total quality control — management by temperature control, use of pesticides and computer/satellite-based logistics. The demand for freshness has also contributed to concerns about food wastage. Use of 'best before', 'sell by' and 'eat by' labels has legally 238)[banned / permitted] institutional waste. Campaigners have 239)[revealed / concealed] the scandal of overproduction and waste. Tristram Stuart, one of the global band of anti-waste campaigners, argues that, with freshly made sandwiches, over-ordering is standard practice across the retail sector to avoid the appearance of empty shelf space, leading to high volumes of waste when supply regularly exceeds demand.

* pesticide: 살충제 ** logistics: 물류, 유통

2022년_고1_9월_인천광역시 교육청_학력평가_34번

12. 다음 글의 괄호 안에서 문맥에 맞는 어휘를 고르시오.

In the studies of Colin Cherry at the Massachusetts Institute for Technology back in the 1950s, his participants listened to voices in one ear at a time and then through both ears in an effort to determine whether we can listen to two people talk 240)[simultaneously / individually]. One ear always contained a message that the listener had to repeat back (called "shadowing") while the other ear included people speaking. The trick was to see if you could totally focus on the main message and also hear someone talking in your other ear. Cleverly, Cherry found it was 241)[possible / impossible] for his participants to know whether the message in the other ear was spoken by a man or woman, in English or another language, or was even comprised of real words at all! In other words, people could not process two pieces of information at the same time.

스승의날 영어연구소

2022년_고1_9월_인천광역시 교육청_학력평가_35번

13. 다음 글의 괄호 안에서 문맥에 맞는 어휘를 고르시오.

The fast-paced 242)[**revolution / evolution**] of Information and Communication Technologies (ICTs) has radically transformed the dynamics and business models of the tourism and hospitality industry. This 243)[**misleads to / results in**] new levels/forms of competitiveness among service providers and transforms the customer experience through new services. Creating unique experiences and providing convenient services to customers leads to 244) [**contentment / dissatisfaction**] and, eventually, customer loyalty to the service provider or brand (i.e., hotels). In particular, the most recent technological boost received by the tourism sector is represented by mobile applications. Indeed, empowering tourists with mobile access to services such as hotel reservations, airline ticketing, and recommendations for local attractions generates strong interest and considerable profits.

* hospitality industry: 서비스업(호텔·식당업 등)

2022년_고1_9월_인천광역시 교육청_학력평가_36번

14. 다음 글의 괄호 안에서 문맥에 맞는 어휘를 고르시오.

With nearly a billion hungry people in the world, there is 245)[**unclearly / plainly**] plainly no single cause. However, far and away the biggest cause is poverty. Seventy-nine percent of the world's hungry live in nations that are net exporters of food. How can this be? The reason people are hungry in those countries is that the products produced there can be sold on the world market for 246)[**less / more**] than the local citizens can afford to pay for them. In the modern age you do not starve because you have no food, you starve 247) [**as / that**] you have no money. So the problem really is that food is, in the grand scheme of things, too expensive and many people are too poor to buy it. The answer will be in continuing the trend of lowering the cost of food.

* net exporter: 순 수출국 ** scheme: 체계, 조직

2022년_고1_9월_인천광역시 교육청_학력평가_37번

15. 다음 글의 괄호 안에서 문맥에 맞는 어휘를 고르시오.

Most people have a perfect time of day when they feel they are at their best, whether in the morning, evening, or afternoon. Some of us are night owls, some early birds, and others in between may feel most 248)[**lazy / active**] during the afternoon hours. If you are able to organize your day and divide your work, make it a point to deal with tasks that demand attention at your best time of the day. However, if the task you face demands creativity and novel ideas, it's best to tackle it at your "worst" time of day! So if you are an early bird, make sure to 249)[**delay / handle**] your creative task in the evening, and vice versa for night owls. When your mind and body are less alert than at your "peak" hours, the muse of creativity 250)[**diminishes / arises**] and is allowed to roam more freely. In other words, when your mental machinery is 251)[**tight / loose**] rather than standing at attention, the creativity flows.

*roam: (어슬렁어슬렁) 거닐다

2022년_고1_9월_인천광역시 교육청_학력평가_38번

16. 다음 글의 괄호 안에서 문맥에 맞는 어휘를 고르시오.

Television is the number one leisure activity in the United States and Europe, consuming more than half of our free time. We generally think of television as a way to relax, tune out, and escape from our troubles for a bit each day. While this is true, there is increasing evidence that we are 252)[**less / more**] motivated to tune in to our favorite shows and characters when we are feeling 253)[**happy / solitary**] or have a greater need for social connection. Television watching does satisfy these social needs to some extent, at least in the short run. Unfortunately, it is also likely to 254)[**include / exclude**] other activities that produce more sustainable social contributions to our social well-being. The more television we watch, the 255)[**more / less**] likely we are to volunteer our time or to spend time with people in our social networks. In other words, the more time we make for Friends, the 256)[**more / less**] time we have for friends in real life.

*Friends: 프렌즈(미국의 한 방송국에서 방영된 시트콤)

2022년_고1_9월_인천광역시 교육청_학력평가_39번

17. 다음 글의 괄호 안에서 문맥에 맞는 어휘를 고르시오.

We often associate the concept of temperature with how hot or cold an object feels when we touch it. In this way, our senses provide us with a qualitative indication of temperature. Our senses, however, are 257)[**reliable** / **incredible**] and often mislead us. For example, if you stand in bare feet with one foot on carpet and the other on a tile floor, the tile feels colder than the carpet even though both are at the 258)[**equal** / **different**] temperature. The two objects feel different because tile transfers energy by heat at a higher rate than carpet does. Your skin "measures" the rate of energy transfer by heat rather than the actual temperature. What we need is a reliable and reproducible method for measuring the 259)[**absolute** / **relative**] hotness or coldness of objects rather than the rate of energy transfer. Scientists have developed a variety of thermometers for making such quantitative measurements.

*thermometer: 온도계

2022년_고1_9월_인천광역시 교육청_학력평가_40번

18. 다음 글의 괄호 안에서 문맥에 맞는 어휘를 고르시오.

My colleagues and I ran an experiment testing two different messages meant to convince thousands of 260)[**willing** / **reluctant**] alumni to make a donation. One message emphasized the opportunity to do good: donating would benefit students, faculty, and staff. The other emphasized the opportunity to feel good: donors would enjoy the warm glow of giving. The two messages were equally effective: in both cases, 6.5 percent of the unwilling alumni ended up donating. Then we combined them, because two reasons are better than one. Except they weren't. When we put the two reasons together, the giving rate dropped below 3 percent. Each reason alone was more than twice as effective as the two combined. The audience was already 261)[**convinced** / **doubtful**]. When we gave them different kinds of reasons to donate, we triggered their awareness that someone was trying to persuade them — and they shielded themselves against it.

* alumni: 졸업생 ** skeptical: 회의적인

2022년_고1_9월_인천광역시 교육청_학력평가_41~42번

19. 다음 글의 괄호 안에서 문맥에 맞는 어휘를 고르시오.

In a society that 262)[**accepts** / **refuses**] the consumption of insects there are some individuals who overcome this rejection, but most will continue with this attitude. It may be very difficult to convince an entire society that insects are totally 263)[**improper** / **proper**] for consumption. However, there are examples in which this reversal of attitudes about certain foods has happened to an entire society. Several examples in the past 120 years from European-American society are: considering lobster a luxury food instead of a food for servants and prisoners; considering sushi a safe and delicious food; and considering pizza not just a food for the rural poor of Sicily. In Latin American countries, where insects are already consumed, a portion of the population 264)[**allows** / **refuses**] their consumption and associates it with poverty. There are also examples of people who have had the habit of consuming them and 265)[**retained** / **discarded**] that habit due to shame, and because they do not want to be categorized as poor or uncivilized. According to Esther Katz, an anthropologist, if the consumption of insects as a food luxury is to be promoted, there would be 266)[**less** / **more**] chances that some individuals who do not present this habit overcome ideas under which they were educated. And this could also help to revalue the consumption of insects by those people who already eat them.

문장 넣기 (A)

2022년_고1_9월_인천광역시 교육청_학력평가_18번

1. 다음 글의 흐름으로 보아, 주어진 문장이 들어가기에 가장 적절한 곳은?267)

Fruit and vegetables are welcomed if they are pre-packed in a sealed packet from the shop.

Dear Parents/Guardians, Class parties will be held on the afternoon December 16th, 2022. (①) Children may bring in sweets, crisps, biscuits, cakes, and drinks. (②) We are requesting that children do not bring in home-cooked or prepared food. All food should arrive in a sealed packet with the ingredients clearly listed. (③) Please DO NOT send any food into school containing nuts as we have many children with severe nut allergies. (④) Please check the ingredients of all food your children bring carefully. (⑤) Thank you for your continued support and cooperation. Yours sincerely, Lisa Brown, Headteacher

2022년_고1_9월_인천광역시 교육청_학력평가_19번

2. 다음 글의 흐름으로 보아, 주어진 문장이 들어가기에 가장 적절한 곳은?268)

After picking it out, I pressed and pulled some parts.

It was two hours before the submission deadline and I still hadn't finished my news article. (①) I sat at the desk, but suddenly, the typewriter didn't work. (②) No matter how hard I tapped the keys, the levers wouldn't move to strike the paper. I started to realize that I would not be able to finish the article on time. (③) Desperately, I rested the typewriter on my lap and started hitting each key with as much force as I could manage. Nothing happened. (④) Thinking something might have happened inside of it, I opened the cover, lifted up the keys, and found the problem — a paper clip. The keys had no room to move. (⑤) The keys moved smoothly again. I breathed deeply and smiled. Now I knew that I could finish my article on time.

2022년_고1_9월_인천광역시 교육청_학력평가_20번

3. 다음 글의 흐름으로 보아, 주어진 문장이 들어가기에 가장 적절한 곳은?269)

Why is this so?

Experts on writing say, "Get rid of as many words as possible." (①) Each word must do something important. If it doesn't, get rid of it. (②) Well, this doesn't work for speaking. It takes more words to introduce, express, and adequately elaborate an idea in speech than it takes in writing. (③) While the reader can reread, the listener cannot rehear. Speakers do not come equipped with a replay button. (④) Because listeners are easily distracted, they will miss many pieces of what a speaker says. If they miss the crucial sentence, they may never catch up. (⑤) This makes it necessary for speakers to talk longer about their points, using more words on them than would be used to express the same idea in writing.

2022년_고1_9월_인천광역시 교육청_학력평가_26번

4. 다음 글의 흐름으로 보아, 주어진 문장이 들어가기에 가장 적절한 곳은?270)

Smith studied further and became a tax accountant, but he finally turned back to his love of writing.

Wilbur Smith was a South African novelist specialising in historical fiction. (①) Smith wanted to become a journalist, writing about social conditions in South Africa, but his father was never supportive of his writing and forced him to get a real job. (②) He wrote his first novel, The Gods First Make Mad, and had received 20 rejections by 1962. (③) In 1964, Smith published another novel, When the Lion Feeds, and it went on to be successful, selling around the world. (④) A famous actor and film producer bought the film rights for When the Lion Feeds, although no movie resulted. (⑤) By the time of his death in 2021 he had published 49 novels, selling more than 140 million copies worldwide.

2022년_고1_9월_인천광역시 교육청_학력평가_30번

5. 다음 글의 흐름으로 보아, 주어진 문장이 들어가기에 가장 적절한 곳은?271)

That can create a temporary feeling of a high, which makes it seem as if your health condition has improved. Also, herbs can have a placebo effect, just like any other method, thus helping you feel better.

It is widely believed that certain herbs somehow magically improve the work of certain organs, and "cure" specific diseases as a result. (①) Such statements are unscientific and groundless. Sometimes herbs appear to work, since they tend to increase your blood circulation in an aggressive attempt by your body to eliminate them from your system. (②) Whatever the case, it is your body that has the intelligence to regain health, and not the herbs. (③) How can herbs have the intelligence needed to direct your body into getting healthier? That is impossible. (④) Try to imagine how herbs might come into your body and intelligently fix your problems. If you try to do that, you will see how impossible it seems. (⑤) Otherwise, it would mean that herbs are more intelligent than the human body, which is truly hard to believe.

*placebo effect: 위약 효과

2022년_고1_9월_인천광역시 교육청_학력평가_31번

6. 다음 글의 흐름으로 보아, 주어진 문장이 들어가기에 가장 적절한 곳은?272)

Working in such conditions reduces people to machines made of flesh.

(①) We worry that the robots are taking our jobs, but just as common a problem is that the robots are taking our judgment. (②) In the large warehouses so common behind the scenes of today's economy, human 'pickers' hurry around grabbing products off shelves and moving them to where they can be packed and dispatched. (③) In their ears are headpieces: the voice of 'Jennifer', a piece of software, tells them where to go and what to do, controlling the smallest details of their movements. (④) Jennifer breaks down instructions into tiny chunks, to minimise error and maximise productivity — for example, rather than picking eighteen copies of a book off a shelf, the human worker would be politely instructed to pick five. Then another five. Then yet another five. Then another three. (⑤) Rather than asking us to think or adapt, the Jennifer unit takes over the thought process and treats workers as an inexpensive source of some visual processing and a pair of opposable thumbs.

*dispatch: 발송하다 **chunk: 덩어리

2022년_고1_9월_인천광역시 교육청_학력평가_32번

7. 다음 글의 흐름으로 보아, 주어진 문장이 들어가기에 가장 적절한 곳은?273)

The infant brings adults into close contact, making one-on-one interactions and creating opportunities for learning.

(①) The prevailing view among developmental scientists is that people are active contributors to their own development. (②) People are influenced by the physical and social contexts in which they live, but they also play a role in influencing their development by interacting with, and changing, those contexts. (③) Even infants influence the world around them and construct their own development through their interactions. (④) Consider an infant who smiles at each adult he sees; he influences his world because adults are likely to smile, use "baby talk," and play with him in response. (⑤) By engaging the world around them, thinking, being curious, and interacting with people, objects, and the world around them, individuals of all ages are "manufacturers of their own development."

2022년_고1_9월_인천광역시 교육청_학력평가_33번

8. 다음 글의 흐름으로 보아, 주어진 문장이 들어가기에 가장 적절한 곳은?274)

The demand for freshness has also contributed to concerns about food wastage.

(①) The demand for freshness can have hidden environmental costs. (②) While freshness is now being used as a term in food marketing as part of a return to nature, the demand for year-round supplies of fresh produce such as soft fruit and exotic vegetables has led to the widespread use of hot houses in cold climates and increasing reliance on total quality control — management by temperature control, use of pesticides and computer/satellite-based logistics. (③) Use of 'best before', 'sell by' and 'eat by' labels has legally allowed institutional waste. (④) Campaigners have exposed the scandal of overproduction and waste. (⑤) Tristram Stuart, one of the global band of anti-waste campaigners, argues that, with freshly made sandwiches, over-ordering is standard practice across the retail sector to avoid the appearance of empty shelf space, leading to high volumes of waste when supply regularly exceeds demand.

* pesticide: 살충제 ** logistics: 물류, 유통

2022년_고1_9월_인천광역시 교육청_학력평가_36번

9. 다음 글의 흐름으로 보아, 주어진 문장이 들어가기에 가장 적절한 곳은?275)

So the problem really is that food is, in the grand scheme of things, too expensive and many people are too poor to buy it.

With nearly a billion hungry people in the world, there is obviously no single cause. (①) However, far and away the biggest cause is poverty. (②) Seventy-nine percent of the world's hungry live in nations that are net exporters of food. (③) How can this be? The reason people are hungry in those countries is that the products produced there can be sold on the world market for more than the local citizens can afford to pay for them. (④) In the modern age you do not starve because you have no food, you starve because you have no money. (⑤) The answer will be in continuing the trend of lowering the cost of food.

* net exporter: 순 수출국 ** scheme: 체계, 조직

2022년_고1_9월_인천광역시 교육청_학력평가_37번

10. 다음 글의 흐름으로 보아, 주어진 문장이 들어가기에 가장 적절한 곳은?276)

So if you are an early bird, make sure to attack your creative task in the evening, and vice versa for night owls.

Most people have a perfect time of day when they feel they are at their best, whether in the morning, evening, or afternoon. (①) Some of us are night owls, some early birds, and others in between may feel most active during the afternoon hours. (②) If you are able to organize your day and divide your work, make it a point to deal with tasks that demand attention at your best time of the day. (③) However, if the task you face demands creativity and novel ideas, it's best to tackle it at your "worst" time of day! (④) When your mind and body are less alert than at your "peak" hours, the muse of creativity awakens and is allowed to roam more freely. (⑤) In other words, when your mental machinery is loose rather than standing at attention, the creativity flows.

*roam: (어슬렁어슬렁) 거닐다

2022년_고1_9월_인천광역시 교육청_학력평가_38번

11. 다음 글의 흐름으로 보아, 주어진 문장이 들어가기에 가장 적절한 곳은?277)

In other words, the more time we make for Friends, the less time we have for friends in real life.

Television is the number one leisure activity in the United States and Europe, consuming more than half of our free time. (①) We generally think of television as a way to relax, tune out, and escape from our troubles for a bit each day. (②) While this is true, there is increasing evidence that we are more motivated to tune in to our favorite shows and characters when we are feeling lonely or have a greater need for social connection. (③) Television watching does satisfy these social needs to some extent, at least in the short run. (④) Unfortunately, it is also likely to "crowd out" other activities that produce more sustainable social contributions to our social well-being. The more television we watch, the less likely we are to volunteer our time or to spend time with people in our social networks. (⑤)

*Friends: 프렌즈(미국의 한 방송국에서 방영된 시트콤)

2022년_고1_9월_인천광역시 교육청_학력평가_39번

12. 다음 글의 흐름으로 보아, 주어진 문장이 들어가기에 가장 적절한 곳은?278)

The two objects feel different because tile transfers energy by heat at a higher rate than carpet does.

We often associate the concept of temperature with how hot or cold an object feels when we touch it. (①) In this way, our senses provide us with a qualitative indication of temperature. (②) Our senses, however, are unreliable and often mislead us. (③) For example, if you stand in bare feet with one foot on carpet and the other on a tile floor, the tile feels colder than the carpet even though both are at the same temperature. (④) Your skin "measures" the rate of energy transfer by heat rather than the actual temperature. (⑤) What we need is a reliable and reproducible method for measuring the relative hotness or coldness of objects rather than the rate of energy transfer. Scientists have developed a variety of thermometers for making such quantitative measurements.

*thermometer: 온도계

2022년_고1_9월_인천광역시 교육청_학력평가_40번

13. 다음 글의 흐름으로 보아, 주어진 문장이 들어가기에 가장 적절한 곳은?279)

Each reason alone was more than twice as effective as the two combined. The audience was already skeptical.

My colleagues and I ran an experiment testing two different messages meant to convince thousands of resistant alumni to make a donation. (①) One message emphasized the opportunity to do good: donating would benefit students, faculty, and staff. (②) The other emphasized the opportunity to feel good: donors would enjoy the warm glow of giving. (③) The two messages were equally effective: in both cases, 6.5 percent of the unwilling alumni ended up donating. (④) Then we combined them, because two reasons are better than one. Except they weren't. When we put the two reasons together, the giving rate dropped below 3 percent. (⑤) When we gave them different kinds of reasons to donate, we triggered their awareness that someone was trying to persuade them — and they shielded themselves against it.

* alumni: 졸업생 ** skeptical: 회의적인

2022년_고1_9월_인천광역시 교육청_학력평가_41~42번

14. 다음 글의 흐름으로 보아, 주어진 문장이 들어가기에 가장 적절한 곳은?280)

There are also examples of people who have had the habit of consuming them and abandoned that habit due to shame, and because they do not want to be categorized as poor or uncivilized.

In a society that rejects the consumption of insects there are some individuals who overcome this rejection, but most will continue with this attitude. It may be very difficult to convince an entire society that insects are totally suitable for consumption. (①) However, there are examples in which this reversal of attitudes about certain foods has happened to an entire society. (②) Several examples in the past 120 years from European-American society are: considering lobster a luxury food instead of a food for servants and prisoners; considering sushi a safe and delicious food; and considering pizza not just a food for the rural poor of Sicily. (③) In Latin American countries, where insects are already consumed, a portion of the population hates their consumption and associates it with poverty. (④) According to Esther Katz, an anthropologist, if the consumption of insects as a food luxury is to be promoted, there would be more chances that some individuals who do not present this habit overcome ideas under which they were educated. (⑤) And this could also help to revalue the consumption of insects by those people who already eat them.

순서 배열(A)

2022년_고1_9월_인천광역시 교육청_학력평가_18번

1. 주어진 글 다음에 이어질 글의 순서로 가장 적절한 것은?281)

Dear Parents/Guardians, Class parties will be held on the afternoon December 16th, 2022.

(A) Children may bring in sweets, crisps, biscuits, cakes, and drinks. We are requesting that children do not bring in home-cooked or prepared food. All food should arrive in a sealed packet with the ingredients clearly listed.

(B) Please check the ingredients of all food your children bring carefully. Thank you for your continued support and cooperation. Yours sincerely, Lisa Brown, Headteacher

(C) Fruit and vegetables are welcomed if they are pre-packed in a sealed packet from the shop. Please DO NOT send any food into school containing nuts as we have many children with severe nut allergies.

① (A) - (C) - (B)   ② (B) - (A) - (C)
③ (B) - (C) - (A)   ④ (C) - (A) - (B)
⑤ (C) - (B) - (A)

2022년_고1_9월_인천광역시 교육청_학력평가_19번

2. 주어진 글 다음에 이어질 글의 순서로 가장 적절한 것은?282)

It was two hours before the submission deadline and I still hadn't finished my news article. I sat at the desk, but suddenly, the typewriter didn't work. No matter how hard I tapped the keys, the levers wouldn't move to strike the paper.

(A) After picking it out, I pressed and pulled some parts. The keys moved smoothly again. I breathed deeply and smiled. Now I knew that I could finish my article on time.

(B) Thinking something might have happened inside of it, I opened the cover, lifted up the keys, and found the problem — a paper clip. The keys had no room to move.

(C) I started to realize that I would not be able to finish the article on time. Desperately, I rested the typewriter on my lap and started hitting each key with as much force as I could manage. Nothing happened.

① (A) - (C) - (B)   ② (B) - (A) - (C)
③ (B) - (C) - (A)   ④ (C) - (A) - (B)
⑤ (C) - (B) - (A)

3. 주어진 글 다음에 이어질 글의 순서로 가장 적절한 것은?283)

Experts on writing say, "Get rid of as many words as possible." Each word must do something important.

(A) This makes it necessary for speakers to talk longer about their points, using more words on them than would be used to express the same idea in writing.

(B) While the reader can reread, the listener cannot rehear. Speakers do not come equipped with a replay button. Because listeners are easily distracted, they will miss many pieces of what a speaker says. If they miss the crucial sentence, they may never catch up.

(C) If it doesn't, get rid of it. Well, this doesn't work for speaking. It takes more words to introduce, express, and adequately elaborate an idea in speech than it takes in writing. Why is this so?

① (A) - (C) - (B) ② (B) - (A) - (C)
③ (B) - (C) - (A) ④ (C) - (A) - (B)
⑤ (C) - (B) - (A)

4. 주어진 글 다음에 이어질 글의 순서로 가장 적절한 것은?284)

Is the customer always right? When customers return a broken product to a famous company, which makes kitchen and bathroom fixtures, the company nearly always offers a replacement to maintain good customer relations.

(A) Entrepreneur Lauren Thorp, who owns an e-commerce company, says, "While the customer is 'always' right, sometimes you just have to fire a customer."

(B) Still, "there are times you've got to say 'no,'" explains the warranty expert of the company, such as when a product is undamaged or has been abused.

(C) When Thorp has tried everything to resolve a complaint and realizes that the customer will be dissatisfied no matter what, she returns her attention to the rest of her customers, who she says are "the reason for my success."

① (A) - (C) - (B) ② (B) - (A) - (C)
③ (B) - (C) - (A) ④ (C) - (A) - (B)
⑤ (C) - (B) - (A)

2022년_고1_9월_인천광역시 교육청_학력평가_22번

5. 주어진 글 다음에 이어질 글의 순서로 가장 적절한 것은?285)

A recent study from Carnegie Mellon University in Pittsburgh, called "When Too Much of a Good Thing May Be Bad," indicates that classrooms with too much decoration are a source of distraction for young children and directly affect their cognitive performance.

(A) On the other hand, if there is not much decoration on the classroom walls, the children are less distracted, spend more time on their activities, and learn more.

(B) Being visually overstimulated, the children have a great deal of difficulty concentrating and end up with worse academic results.

(C) So it's our job, in order to support their attention, to find the right balance between excessive decoration and the complete absence of it.

① (A) - (C) - (B)　　② (B) - (A) - (C)
③ (B) - (C) - (A)　　④ (C) - (A) - (B)
⑤ (C) - (B) - (A)

2022년_고1_9월_인천광역시 교육청_학력평가_23번

6. 주어진 글 다음에 이어질 글의 순서로 가장 적절한 것은?286)

For creatures like us, evolution smiled upon those with a strong need to belong.

(A) In particular, if an individual and a group want the same resource, the group will generally prevail, so competition for resources would especially favor a need to belong.

(B) Survival and reproduction are the criteria of success by natural selection, and forming relationships with other people can be useful for both survival and reproduction. Groups can share resources, care for sick members, scare off predators, fight together against enemies, divide tasks so as to improve efficiency, and contribute to survival in many other ways.

(C) Belongingness will likewise promote reproduction, such as by bringing potential mates into contact with each other, and in particular by keeping parents together to care for their children, who are much more likely to survive if they have more than one caregiver.

① (A) - (C) - (B)　　② (B) - (A) - (C)
③ (B) - (C) - (A)　　④ (C) - (A) - (B)
⑤ (C) - (B) - (A)

2022년_고1_9월_인천광역시 교육청_학력평가_24번

7. 주어진 글 다음에 이어질 글의 순서로 가장 적절한 것은?287)

Many people make a mistake of only operating along the safe zones, and in the process they miss the opportunity to achieve greater things.

(A) Being overcautious will mean that you will miss attaining the greatest levels of your potential.

(B) You must learn to take those chances that many people around you will not take, because your success will flow from those bold decisions that you will take along the way.

(C) They do so because of a fear of the unknown and a fear of treading the unknown paths of life. Those that are brave enough to take those roads less travelled are able to get great returns and derive major satisfaction out of their courageous moves.

*tread: 밟다

① (A) - (C) - (B) ② (B) - (A) - (C)
③ (B) - (C) - (A) ④ (C) - (A) - (B)
⑤ (C) - (B) - (A)

2022년_고1_9월_인천광역시 교육청_학력평가_26번

8. 주어진 글 다음에 이어질 글의 순서로 가장 적절한 것은?288)

Wilbur Smith was a South African novelist specialising in historical fiction. Smith wanted to become a journalist, writing about social conditions in South Africa, but his father was never supportive of his writing and forced him to get a real job.

(A) A famous actor and film producer bought the film rights for When the Lion Feeds, although no movie resulted.

(B) By the time of his death in 2021 he had published 49 novels, selling more than 140 million copies worldwide.

(C) Smith studied further and became a tax accountant, but he finally turned back to his love of writing. He wrote his first novel, The Gods First Make Mad, and had received 20 rejections by 1962. In 1964, Smith published another novel, When the Lion Feeds, and it went on to be successful, selling around the world.

① (A) - (C) - (B) ② (B) - (A) - (C)
③ (B) - (C) - (A) ④ (C) - (A) - (B)
⑤ (C) - (B) - (A)

2022년_고1_9월_인천광역시 교육청_학력평가_29번

9. 주어진 글 다음에 이어질 글의 순서로 가장 적절한 것은?289)

The human brain, it turns out, has shrunk in mass by about 10 percent since it peaked in size 15,000-30,000 years ago.

(A) One possible reason is that many thousands of years ago humans lived in a world of dangerous predators where they had to have their wits about them at all times to avoid being killed.

(B) None of this may mean we are dumber — brain size is not necessarily an indicator of human intelligence — but it may mean that our brains today are wired up differently, and perhaps more efficiently, than those of our ancestors.

(C) Today, we have effectively domesticated ourselves and many of the tasks of survival — from avoiding immediate death to building shelters to obtaining food — have been outsourced to the wider society. We are smaller than our ancestors too, and it is a characteristic of domestic animals that they are generally smaller than their wild cousins.

① (A) - (C) - (B) ② (B) - (A) - (C)
③ (B) - (C) - (A) ④ (C) - (A) - (B)
⑤ (C) - (B) - (A)

2022년_고1_9월_인천광역시 교육청_학력평가_30번

10. 주어진 글 다음에 이어질 글의 순서로 가장 적절한 것은?290)

It is widely believed that certain herbs somehow magically improve the work of certain organs, and "cure" specific diseases as a result. Such statements are unscientific and groundless.

(A) Otherwise, it would mean that herbs are more intelligent than the human body, which is truly hard to believe.

(B) Sometimes herbs appear to work, since they tend to increase your blood circulation in an aggressive attempt by your body to eliminate them from your system. That can create a temporary feeling of a high, which makes it seem as if your health condition has improved.

(C) Also, herbs can have a placebo effect, just like any other method, thus helping you feel better. Whatever the case, it is your body that has the intelligence to regain health, and not the herbs. How can herbs have the intelligence needed to direct your body into getting healthier? That is impossible. Try to imagine how herbs might come into your body and intelligently fix your problems. If you try to do that, you will see how impossible it seems.

*placebo effect: 위약 효과

① (A) - (C) - (B) ② (B) - (A) - (C)
③ (B) - (C) - (A) ④ (C) - (A) - (B)
⑤ (C) - (B) - (A)

스승의날 영어연구소

2022년_고1_9월_인천광역시 교육청_학력평가_31번

11. 주어진 글 다음에 이어질 글의 순서로 가장 적절한 것은?291)

We worry that the robots are taking our jobs, but just as common a problem is that the robots are taking our judgment.

(A) In their ears are headpieces: the voice of 'Jennifer', a piece of software, tells them where to go and what to do, controlling the smallest details of their movements. Jennifer breaks down instructions into tiny chunks, to minimise error and maximise productivity — for example, rather than picking eighteen copies of a book off a shelf, the human worker would be politely instructed to pick five. Then another five. Then yet another five. Then another three. Working in such conditions reduces people to machines made of flesh.

(B) Rather than asking us to think or adapt, the Jennifer unit takes over the thought process and treats workers as an inexpensive source of some visual processing and a pair of opposable thumbs.

(C) In the large warehouses so common behind the scenes of today's economy, human 'pickers' hurry around grabbing products off shelves and moving them to where they can be packed and dispatched.

*dispatch: 발송하다 **chunk: 덩어리

① (A) - (C) - (B)　　② (B) - (A) - (C)
③ (B) - (C) - (A)　　④ (C) - (A) - (B)
⑤ (C) - (B) - (A)

2022년_고1_9월_인천광역시 교육청_학력평가_32번

12. 주어진 글 다음에 이어질 글의 순서로 가장 적절한 것은?292)

The prevailing view among developmental scientists is that people are active contributors to their own development.

(A) People are influenced by the physical and social contexts in which they live, but they also play a role in influencing their development by interacting with, and changing, those contexts.

(B) By engaging the world around them, thinking, being curious, and interacting with people, objects, and the world around them, individuals of all ages are "manufacturers of their own development."

(C) Even infants influence the world around them and construct their own development through their interactions. Consider an infant who smiles at each adult he sees; he influences his world because adults are likely to smile, use "baby talk," and play with him in response. The infant brings adults into close contact, making one-on-one interactions and creating opportunities for learning.

① (A) - (C) - (B)　　② (B) - (A) - (C)
③ (B) - (C) - (A)　　④ (C) - (A) - (B)
⑤ (C) - (B) - (A)

2022년_고1_9월_인천광역시 교육청_학력평가_33번

13. 주어진 글 다음에 이어질 글의 순서로 가장 적절한 것은?293)

The demand for freshness can have hidden environmental costs.

(A) While freshness is now being used as a term in food marketing as part of a return to nature, the demand for year-round supplies of fresh produce such as soft fruit and exotic vegetables has led to the widespread use of hot houses in cold climates and increasing reliance on total quality control — management by temperature control, use of pesticides and computer/satellite-based logistics.

(B) Tristram Stuart, one of the global band of anti-waste campaigners, argues that, with freshly made sandwiches, over-ordering is standard practice across the retail sector to avoid the appearance of empty shelf space, leading to high volumes of waste when supply regularly exceeds demand.

(C) The demand for freshness has also contributed to concerns about food wastage. Use of 'best before', 'sell by' and 'eat by' labels has legally allowed institutional waste. Campaigners have exposed the scandal of overproduction and waste.

* pesticide: 살충제 ** logistics: 물류, 유통

① (A) - (C) - (B) ② (B) - (A) - (C)
③ (B) - (C) - (A) ④ (C) - (A) - (B)
⑤ (C) - (B) - (A)

2022년_고1_9월_인천광역시 교육청_학력평가_34번

14. 주어진 글 다음에 이어질 글의 순서로 가장 적절한 것은?294)

In the studies of Colin Cherry at the Massachusetts Institute for Technology back in the 1950s, his participants listened to voices in one ear at a time and then through both ears in an effort to determine whether we can listen to two people talk at the same time.

(A) One ear always contained a message that the listener had to repeat back (called "shadowing") while the other ear included people speaking.

(B) In other words, people could not process two pieces of information at the same time.

(C) The trick was to see if you could totally focus on the main message and also hear someone talking in your other ear. Cleverly, Cherry found it was impossible for his participants to know whether the message in the other ear was spoken by a man or woman, in English or another language, or was even comprised of real words at all!

① (A) - (C) - (B) ② (B) - (A) - (C)
③ (B) - (C) - (A) ④ (C) - (A) - (B)
⑤ (C) - (B) - (A)

15. 주어진 글 다음에 이어질 글의 순서로 가장 적절한 것은?295)

The fast-paced evolution of Information and Communication Technologies (ICTs) has radically transformed the dynamics and business models of the tourism and hospitality industry.

(A) This leads to new levels/forms of competitiveness among service providers and transforms the customer experience through new services. Creating unique experiences and providing convenient services to customers leads to satisfaction and, eventually, customer loyalty to the service provider or brand (i.e., hotels).

(B) Indeed, empowering tourists with mobile access to services such as hotel reservations, airline ticketing, and recommendations for local attractions generates strong interest and considerable profits.

(C) In particular, the most recent technological boost received by the tourism sector is represented by mobile applications.

　　* hospitality industry: 서비스업(호텔·식당업 등)

① (A) - (C) - (B)　　② (B) - (A) - (C)
③ (B) - (C) - (A)　　④ (C) - (A) - (B)
⑤ (C) - (B) - (A)

16. 주어진 글 다음에 이어질 글의 순서로 가장 적절한 것은?296)

With nearly a billion hungry people in the world, there is obviously no single cause.

(A) The answer will be in continuing the trend of lowering the cost of food.

(B) However, far and away the biggest cause is poverty. Seventy-nine percent of the world's hungry live in nations that are net exporters of food. How can this be?

(C) The reason people are hungry in those countries is that the products produced there can be sold on the world market for more than the local citizens can afford to pay for them. In the modern age you do not starve because you have no food, you starve because you have no money. So the problem really is that food is, in the grand scheme of things, too expensive and many people are too poor to buy it.

　　* net exporter: 순 수출국 ** scheme: 체계, 조직

① (A) - (C) - (B)　　② (B) - (A) - (C)
③ (B) - (C) - (A)　　④ (C) - (A) - (B)
⑤ (C) - (B) - (A)

영어 영역

2022년_고1_9월_인천광역시 교육청_학력평가_37번

17. 주어진 글 다음에 이어질 글의 순서로 가장 적절한 것은?297)

Most people have a perfect time of day when they feel they are at their best, whether in the morning, evening, or afternoon. Some of us are night owls, some early birds, and others in between may feel most active during the afternoon hours.

(A) If you are able to organize your day and divide your work, make it a point to deal with tasks that demand attention at your best time of the day.

(B) In other words, when your mental machinery is loose rather than standing at attention, the creativity flows.

(C) However, if the task you face demands creativity and novel ideas, it's best to tackle it at your "worst" time of day! So if you are an early bird, make sure to attack your creative task in the evening, and vice versa for night owls. When your mind and body are less alert than at your "peak" hours, the muse of creativity awakens and is allowed to roam more freely.

*roam: (어슬렁어슬렁) 거닐다

① (A) - (C) - (B)　　② (B) - (A) - (C)
③ (B) - (C) - (A)　　④ (C) - (A) - (B)
⑤ (C) - (B) - (A)

2022년_고1_9월_인천광역시 교육청_학력평가_38번

18. 주어진 글 다음에 이어질 글의 순서로 가장 적절한 것은?298)

Television is the number one leisure activity in the United States and Europe, consuming more than half of our free time. We generally think of television as a way to relax, tune out, and escape from our troubles for a bit each day.

(A) Unfortunately, it is also likely to "crowd out" other activities that produce more sustainable social contributions to our social well-being. The more television we watch, the less likely we are to volunteer our time or to spend time with people in our social networks.

(B) While this is true, there is increasing evidence that we are more motivated to tune in to our favorite shows and characters when we are feeling lonely or have a greater need for social connection. Television watching does satisfy these social needs to some extent, at least in the short run.

(C) In other words, the more time we make for Friends, the less time we have for friends in real life.

*Friends: 프렌즈(미국의 한 방송국에서 방영된 시트콤)

① (A) - (C) - (B)　　② (B) - (A) - (C)
③ (B) - (C) - (A)　　④ (C) - (A) - (B)
⑤ (C) - (B) - (A)

2022년_고1_9월_인천광역시 교육청_학력평가_39번

19. 주어진 글 다음에 이어질 글의 순서로 가장 적절한 것은?299)

We often associate the concept of temperature with how hot or cold an object feels when we touch it. In this way, our senses provide us with a qualitative indication of temperature.

(A) Your skin "measures" the rate of energy transfer by heat rather than the actual temperature. What we need is a reliable and reproducible method for measuring the relative hotness or coldness of objects rather than the rate of energy transfer.

(B) Our senses, however, are unreliable and often mislead us. For example, if you stand in bare feet with one foot on carpet and the other on a tile floor, the tile feels colder than the carpet even though both are at the same temperature. The two objects feel different because tile transfers energy by heat at a higher rate than carpet does.

(C) Scientists have developed a variety of thermometers for making such quantitative measurements.

*thermometer: 온도계

① (A) - (C) - (B) ② (B) - (A) - (C)
③ (B) - (C) - (A) ④ (C) - (A) - (B)
⑤ (C) - (B) - (A)

2022년_고1_9월_인천광역시 교육청_학력평가_40번

20. 주어진 글 다음에 이어질 글의 순서로 가장 적절한 것은?300)

My colleagues and I ran an experiment testing two different messages meant to convince thousands of resistant alumni to make a donation.

(A) Then we combined them, because two reasons are better than one. Except they weren't. When we put the two reasons together, the giving rate dropped below 3 percent. Each reason alone was more than twice as effective as the two combined.

(B) One message emphasized the opportunity to do good: donating would benefit students, faculty, and staff. The other emphasized the opportunity to feel good: donors would enjoy the warm glow of giving. The two messages were equally effective: in both cases, 6.5 percent of the unwilling alumni ended up donating.

(C) The audience was already skeptical. When we gave them different kinds of reasons to donate, we triggered their awareness that someone was trying to persuade them — and they shielded themselves against it.

* alumni: 졸업생 ** skeptical: 회의적인

① (A) - (C) - (B) ② (B) - (A) - (C)
③ (B) - (C) - (A) ④ (C) - (A) - (B)
⑤ (C) - (B) - (A)

2022년_고1_9월_인천광역시 교육청_학력평가_41~42번

21. 주어진 글 다음에 이어질 글의 순서로 가장 적절한 것은?301)

In a society that rejects the consumption of insects there are some individuals who overcome this rejection, but most will continue with this attitude.

(A) In Latin American countries, where insects are already consumed, a portion of the population hates their consumption and associates it with poverty. There are also examples of people who have had the habit of consuming them and abandoned that habit due to shame, and because they do not want to be categorized as poor or uncivilized.

(B) According to Esther Katz, an anthropologist, if the consumption of insects as a food luxury is to be promoted, there would be more chances that some individuals who do not present this habit overcome ideas under which they were educated. And this could also help to revalue the consumption of insects by those people who already eat them.

(C) It may be very difficult to convince an entire society that insects are totally suitable for consumption. However, there are examples in which this reversal of attitudes about certain foods has happened to an entire society. Several examples in the past 120 years from European-American society are: considering lobster a luxury food instead of a food for servants and prisoners; considering sushi a safe and delicious food; and considering pizza not just a food for the rural poor of Sicily.

① (A) - (C) - (B) ② (B) - (A) - (C)
③ (B) - (C) - (A) ④ (C) - (A) - (B)
⑤ (C) - (B) - (A)

2022년_고1_9월_인천광역시 교육청_학력평가_43~45번

22. 주어진 글 다음에 이어질 글의 순서로 가장 적절한 것은?302)

A boy had a place at the best school in town. In the morning, his granddad took him to the school. When he went onto the playground with his grandson, the children surrounded them. "What a funny old man," one boy smirked. A girl with brown hair pointed at the pair and jumped up and down.

(A) Granddad took his grandson back to his own house, asked grandma to look after him, and went off to look for a teacher himself. Every time he spotted a school, the old man went onto the playground, and waited for the children to come out at break time. In some schools the children completely ignored the old man and in others, they made fun of him. When this happened, he would turn sadly and go home. Finally, he went onto the tiny playground of a very small school, and leant against the fence, exhausted. The bell rang, and the crowd of children ran out onto the playground. "Sir, are you all right? Shall I bring you a glass of water?" a voice said. "We've got a bench in the playground—come and sit down," another voice said. Soon a young teacher came out onto the playground. The old man greeted him and said: "Finally, I've found my grandson the best school in town." "You're mistaken, sir. Our school is not the best —it's small and cramped."

(B) The old man didn't argue with the teacher. Instead, he made arrangements for his grandson to join the school, and then the old man left. That evening, the boy's mom said to him: "Dad, you can't even read. How do you know you've found the best teacher of all?" "Judge a teacher by his pupils," the old man replied.

(C) Suddenly, the bell rang and the children ran off to their first lesson. The old man took his grandson firmly by the hand, and led him out of the school gate. "Brilliant, I don't have to go to school!" the boy exclaimed. "You do, but not this one," his granddad replied. "I'll find you a school myself."

* smirk: 히죽히죽 웃다 * cramped: 비좁은

① (A) - (C) - (B) ② (B) - (A) - (C)
③ (B) - (C) - (A) ④ (C) - (A) - (B)
⑤ (C) - (B) - (A)

연결어 선택(객관식)

2022년_고1_9월_인천광역시 교육청_학력평가_22번

1. 위 글의 빈칸 (A), (B)에 들어갈 말로 가장 적절한 것은?303)

A recent study from Carnegie Mellon University in Pittsburgh, called "When Too Much of a Good Thing May Be Bad," indicates that classrooms with too much decoration are a source of distraction for young children and directly affect their cognitive performance. Being visually overstimulated, the children have a great deal of difficulty concentrating and end up with worse academic results. (A)_____, if there is not much decoration on the classroom walls, the children are less distracted, spend more time on their activities, and learn more. (B)_____ it's our job, in order to support their attention, to find the right balance between excessive decoration and the complete absence of it.

	(A)	(B)
①	Hence	In other words
②	In fact	Hence
③	In fact	In other words
④	However	Hence
⑤	On the other hand	In fact

2022년_고1_9월_인천광역시 교육청_학력평가_23번

2. 위 글의 빈칸 (A), (B)에 들어갈 말로 가장 적절한 것은?304)

For creatures like us, evolution smiled upon those with a strong need to belong. Survival and reproduction are the criteria of success by natural selection, and forming relationships with other people can be useful for both survival and reproduction. Groups can share resources, care for sick members, scare off predators, fight together against enemies, divide tasks so as to improve efficiency, and contribute to survival in many other ways. In particular, if an individual and a group want the same resource, the group will generally prevail, (A)_____ competition for resources would especially favor a need to belong. Belongingness will (B)_____ promote reproduction, such as by bringing potential mates into contact with each other, and in particular by keeping parents together to care for their children, who are much more likely to survive if they have more than one caregiver.

	(A)	(B)
①	However	Therefore
②	However	Similarly
③	Therefore	Therefore
④	Therefore	Similarly
⑤	In addition	Actually

2022년_고1_9월_인천광역시 교육청_학력평가_30

3. 위 글의 빈칸 (A), (B)에 들어갈 말로 가장 적절한 것은?305)

It is widely believed that certain herbs somehow magically improve the work of certain organs, and "cure" specific diseases as a result. Such statements are unscientific and groundless. Sometimes herbs appear to work, since they tend to increase your blood circulation in an aggressive attempt by your body to eliminate them from your system. That can create a temporary feeling of a high, which makes it seem as if your health condition has improved. **(A)**_____, herbs can have a placebo effect, just like any other method, thus helping you feel better. Whatever the case, it is your body that has the intelligence to regain health, and not the herbs. How can herbs have the intelligence needed to direct your body into getting healthier? That is impossible. Try to imagine how herbs might come into your body and intelligently fix your problems. If you try to do that, you will see how impossible it seems. **(B)**_____ , it would mean that herbs are more intelligent than the human body, which is truly hard to believe.

*placebo effect: 위약 효과

	(A)	(B)
①	Also	Therefore
②	Besides	Therefore
③	For example	Likewise
④	Besides	Otherwise
⑤	As a result	Likewise

2022년_고1_9월_인천광역시 교육청_학력평가_34번

4. 위 글의 빈칸 (A), (B)에 들어갈 말로 가장 적절한 것은?306)

In the studies of Colin Cherry at the Massachusetts Institute for Technology back in the 1950s, his participants listened to voices in one ear at a time and then through both ears in an effort to determine whether we can listen to two people talk at the same time. One ear always contained a message that the listener had to repeat back (called "shadowing") while the other ear included people speaking. The trick was to see if you could totally focus on the main message and **(A)**_____ hear someone talking in your other ear. Cleverly, Cherry found it was impossible for his participants to know whether the message in the other ear was spoken by a man or woman, in English or another language, or was even comprised of real words at all! **(B)**_____ , people could not process two pieces of information at the same time.

	(A)	(B)
①	however	In other words
②	however	For example
③	also	In other words
④	hence	On the other hand
⑤	in fact	On the other hand

2022년_고1_9월_인천광역시 교육청_학력평가_36번

5. 위 글의 빈칸 (A), (B)에 들어갈 말로 가장 적절한 것은?307)

With nearly a billion hungry people in the world, there is obviously no single cause. **(A)_____**, far and away the biggest cause is poverty. Seventy-nine percent of the world's hungry live in nations that are net exporters of food. How can this be? The reason people are hungry in those countries is that the products produced there can be sold on the world market for more than the local citizens can afford to pay for them. In the modern age you do not starve because you have no food, you starve because you have no money. **(B)_____** the problem really is that food is, in the grand scheme of things, too expensive and many people are too poor to buy it. The answer will be in continuing the trend of lowering the cost of food.

　　　* net exporter: 순 수출국 ** scheme: 체계, 조직

	(A)	(B)
①	But	So
②	But	In fact
③	For example	Therefore
④	For example	In fact
⑤	As a result	Therefore

2022년_고1_9월_인천광역시 교육청_학력평가_37번

6. 위 글의 빈칸 (A), (B)에 들어갈 말로 가장 적절한 것은?308)

Most people have a perfect time of day when they feel they are at their best, whether in the morning, evening, or afternoon. Some of us are night owls, some early birds, and others in between may feel most active during the afternoon hours. If you are able to organize your day and divide your work, make it a point to deal with tasks that demand attention at your best time of the day. **(A)_____**, if the task you face demands creativity and novel ideas, it's best to tackle it at your "worst" time of day! So if you are an early bird, make sure to attack your creative task in the evening, and vice versa for night owls. When your mind and body are less alert than at your "peak" hours, the muse of creativity awakens and is allowed to roam more freely. **(B)_____**, when your mental machinery is loose rather than standing at attention, the creativity flows.

　　　*roam: (어슬렁어슬렁) 거닐다

	(A)	(B)
①	But	Therefore
②	But	That is to say
③	Therefore	Therefore
④	Therefore	That is to say
⑤	In addition	Actually

어법 Lv_기본(객관식)

2022년_고1_9월_인천광역시 교육청_학력평가_18번

1. 밑줄 친 부분 중, 어법상 틀린 개수를 고르고 틀린 부분은 올바르게 고치시오.309)

Dear Parents/Guardians, Class parties will be ⓐ <u>held</u> on the afternoon December 16th, 2022. Children may ⓑ <u>bring</u> in sweets, crisps, biscuits, cakes, and drinks. We are requesting ⓒ <u>what</u> children do not bring in home-cooked or prepared food. All food should arrive in a sealed packet with the ingredients clearly listed. Fruit and vegetables are welcomed ⓓ <u>if</u> they are pre-packed in a sealed packet from the shop. Please DO NOT send any food into school ⓔ <u>contained</u> nuts as we have many children with severe nut allergies. Please check the ingredients of all food your children bring ⓕ <u>carefully</u>. Thank you for your continued support and cooperation. Yours sincerely, Lisa Brown, Headteacher

① 1개　② 2개　③ 3개　④ 4개　⑤ 5개

ⓐ: _____ → _____

ⓑ: _____ → _____

ⓒ: _____ → _____

ⓓ: _____ → _____

ⓔ: _____ → _____

ⓕ: _____ → _____

2022년_고1_9월_인천광역시 교육청_학력평가_19번

2. 밑줄 친 부분 중, 어법상 틀린 개수를 고르고 틀린 부분은 올바르게 고치시오.310)

It was two hours before the submission deadline and I still ⓐ <u>hadn't</u> finished my news article. I sat at the desk, but suddenly, the typewriter didn't work. No matter how ⓑ <u>hard I tapped</u> the keys, the levers wouldn't move to strike the paper. I started to realize ⓒ <u>that</u> I would not be able to finish the article on time. Desperately, I rested the typewriter on my lap and started hitting each key with as much force as I could ⓓ <u>be managed</u>. Nothing happened. Thinking something might ⓔ <u>happen</u> inside of it, I opened the cover, lifted up the keys, and found the problem — a paper clip. The keys had no room to move. After picking it out, I pressed and pulled some parts. The keys moved ⓕ <u>smooth</u> again. I breathed deeply and smiled. Now I knew that I could finish my article on time.

① 1개　② 2개　③ 3개　④ 4개　⑤ 5개

ⓐ: _____ → _____

ⓑ: _____ → _____

ⓒ: _____ → _____

ⓓ: _____ → _____

ⓔ: _____ → _____

ⓕ: _____ → _____

2022년_고1_9월_인천광역시 교육청_학력평가_20번

3. 밑줄 친 부분 중, 어법상 틀린 개수를 고르고 틀린 부분은 올바르게 고치시오.311)

Experts on writing say, "Get rid of as many words as possible." Each ⓐ <u>words</u> must do something important. If it ⓑ <u>isn't</u>, get rid of it. Well, this doesn't work for speaking. It takes more words to introduce, express, and adequately elaborate an idea in speech than it takes in writing. Why is this so? ⓒ <u>While</u> the reader can reread, the listener cannot rehear. Speakers do not come ⓓ <u>equipping</u> with a replay button. Because listeners are easily ⓔ <u>distracting</u>, they will miss many pieces of what a speaker says. If they miss the crucial sentence, they may never catch up. This makes it necessary for speakers to talk longer about their points, ⓕ <u>using</u> more words on them than would be used to express the same idea in writing.

① 1개 ② 2개 ③ 3개 ④ 4개 ⑤ 5개

ⓐ: ＿＿＿＿＿＿＿ → ＿＿＿＿＿＿＿

ⓑ: ＿＿＿＿＿＿＿ → ＿＿＿＿＿＿＿

ⓒ: ＿＿＿＿＿＿＿ → ＿＿＿＿＿＿＿

ⓓ: ＿＿＿＿＿＿＿ → ＿＿＿＿＿＿＿

ⓔ: ＿＿＿＿＿＿＿ → ＿＿＿＿＿＿＿

ⓕ: ＿＿＿＿＿＿＿ → ＿＿＿＿＿＿＿

2022년_고1_9월_인천광역시 교육청_학력평가_21번

4. 밑줄 친 부분 중, 어법상 틀린 개수를 고르고 틀린 부분은 올바르게 고치시오.312)

Is the customer always right? When customers return a ⓐ <u>broken</u> product to a famous company, ⓑ <u>where</u> makes kitchen and bathroom fixtures, the company nearly always offers a replacement to maintain good customer relations. Still, "there are times you've got to ⓒ <u>say</u> 'no,'" explains the warranty expert of the company, such as when a product is undamaged or has been ⓓ <u>abusing</u>. Entrepreneur Lauren Thorp, who owns an e-commerce company, says, "ⓔ <u>While</u> the customer is 'always' right, sometimes you just have to fire a customer." When Thorp has tried everything to resolve a complaint and realizes that the customer will be dissatisfied no matter what, she returns her attention to the rest of her customers, who she says ⓕ <u>is</u> "the reason for my success."

① 1개 ② 2개 ③ 3개 ④ 4개 ⑤ 5개

ⓐ: ＿＿＿＿＿＿＿ → ＿＿＿＿＿＿＿

ⓑ: ＿＿＿＿＿＿＿ → ＿＿＿＿＿＿＿

ⓒ: ＿＿＿＿＿＿＿ → ＿＿＿＿＿＿＿

ⓓ: ＿＿＿＿＿＿＿ → ＿＿＿＿＿＿＿

ⓔ: ＿＿＿＿＿＿＿ → ＿＿＿＿＿＿＿

ⓕ: ＿＿＿＿＿＿＿ → ＿＿＿＿＿＿＿

2022년_고1_9월_인천광역시 교육청_학력평가_22번

5. 밑줄 친 부분 중, 어법상 틀린 개수를 고르고 틀린 부분은 올바르게 고치시오. 313)

A recent study from Carnegie Mellon University in Pittsburgh, called "When Too Much of a Good Thing May Be Bad," indicates that classrooms with too much decoration are a source of distraction for young children and ⓐ <u>directly</u> affect their cognitive performance. ⓑ <u>Being</u> visually overstimulated, the children have a great deal of difficulty ⓒ <u>concentrate</u> and end up with worse academic results. On the other hand, ⓓ <u>if</u> there is not much decoration on the classroom walls, the children are less ⓔ <u>distracting</u>, spend more time on their activities, and learn more. So it's our job, in order to ⓕ <u>support</u> their attention, to find the right balance between excessive decoration and the complete absence of it.

① 1개　② 2개　③ 3개　④ 4개　⑤ 5개

ⓐ: _____ → _____

ⓑ: _____ → _____

ⓒ: _____ → _____

ⓓ: _____ → _____

ⓔ: _____ → _____

ⓕ: _____ → _____

2022년_고1_9월_인천광역시 교육청_학력평가_23번

6. 밑줄 친 부분 중, 어법상 틀린 개수를 고르고 틀린 부분은 올바르게 고치시오. 314)

For creatures like us, evolution smiled upon those with a strong need to belong. Survival and reproduction are the criteria of success by natural selection, and forming relationships with other people can be ⓐ <u>useful</u> for both survival and reproduction. Groups can ⓑ <u>be shared</u> resources, care for sick members, scare off predators, fight together against enemies, divide tasks so as to improve efficiency, and ⓒ <u>contribute</u> to survival in many other ways. In particular, if an individual and a group want the same resource, the group will generally prevail, so competition for resources would especially favor a need to belong. Belongingness will likewise ⓓ <u>promote</u> reproduction, such as by ⓔ <u>bringing</u> potential mates into contact with each other, and in particular by keeping parents together to care for their children, ⓕ <u>what</u> are much more likely to survive if they have more than one caregiver.

① 1개　② 2개　③ 3개　④ 4개　⑤ 5개

ⓐ: _____ → _____

ⓑ: _____ → _____

ⓒ: _____ → _____

ⓓ: _____ → _____

ⓔ: _____ → _____

ⓕ: _____ → _____

2022년_고1_9월_인천광역시 교육청_학력평가_24번

7. 밑줄 친 부분 중, 어법상 틀린 개수를 고르고 틀린 부분은 올바르게 고치시오.315)

Many people make a mistake of only operating along the safe zones, and in the process they miss the opportunity to achieve greater things. They ⓐ <u>are</u> so because of a fear of the unknown and a fear of treading the unknown paths of life. Those that are ⓑ <u>brave enough</u> to take those roads less ⓒ <u>travelled</u> are able to get great returns and derive major satisfaction out of their courageous moves. Being overcautious will mean ⓓ <u>which</u> you will miss attaining the greatest levels of your potential. You must learn to take those chances ⓔ <u>what</u> many people around you will not take, because your success will ⓕ <u>be flowed</u> from those bold decisions that you will take along the way.

① 1개　② 2개　③ 3개　④ 4개　⑤ 5개

ⓐ: _____ → _____

ⓑ: _____ → _____

ⓒ: _____ → _____

ⓓ: _____ → _____

ⓔ: _____ → _____

ⓕ: _____ → _____

2022년_고1_9월_인천광역시 교육청_학력평가_25번

8. 밑줄 친 부분 중, 어법상 틀린 개수를 고르고 틀린 부분은 올바르게 고치시오.316)

The graph above shows the share of the urban population by continent in 1950 and in 2020. For each ⓐ <u>continent</u>, the share of the urban population in 2020 was larger than that in 1950. From 1950 to 2020, the share of the urban population in Africa ⓑ <u>was increased</u> from 14.3% to 43.5%. The share of the urban population in Asia ⓒ <u>was</u> the second lowest in 1950 but not in 2020. In 1950, the share of the urban population in Europe was larger than ⓓ <u>that</u> in Latin America and the Caribbean, whereas the reverse was true in 2020. Among the five continents, Northern America was ⓔ <u>ranked</u> in the first position for the share of the urban population in both 1950 and 2020.

① 1개　② 2개　③ 3개　④ 4개　⑤ 5개

ⓐ: _____ → _____

ⓑ: _____ → _____

ⓒ: _____ → _____

ⓓ: _____ → _____

ⓔ: _____ → _____

ⓕ: _____ → _____

9. 밑줄 친 부분 중, 어법상 틀린 개수를 고르고 틀린 부분은 올바르게 고치시오.317)

Wilbur Smith was a South African novelist specialising in historical fiction. Smith wanted to become a journalist, ⓐ <u>written</u> about social conditions in South Africa, but his father was never supportive of his writing and forced him ⓑ <u>getting</u> a real job. Smith studied further and became a tax accountant, but he finally turned back to his love of writing. He wrote his first novel, The Gods First Make Mad, and ⓒ <u>had</u> received 20 rejections by 1962. In 1964, Smith ⓓ <u>published</u> another novel, When the Lion Feeds, and it went on to be successful, ⓔ <u>sold</u> around the world. A famous actor and film producer bought the film rights for When the Lion Feeds, although no movie ⓕ <u>was resulted</u>. By the time of his death in 2021 he had published 49 novels, selling more than 140 million copies worldwide.

① 1개　② 2개　③ 3개　④ 4개　⑤ 5개

ⓐ: ＿＿＿＿＿＿ → ＿＿＿＿＿＿

ⓑ: ＿＿＿＿＿＿ → ＿＿＿＿＿＿

ⓒ: ＿＿＿＿＿＿ → ＿＿＿＿＿＿

ⓓ: ＿＿＿＿＿＿ → ＿＿＿＿＿＿

ⓔ: ＿＿＿＿＿＿ → ＿＿＿＿＿＿

ⓕ: ＿＿＿＿＿＿ → ＿＿＿＿＿＿

10. 밑줄 친 부분 중, 어법상 틀린 개수를 고르고 틀린 부분은 올바르게 고치시오.318)

The human brain, it turns out, has ⓐ <u>been shrunk</u> in mass by about 10 percent since it peaked in size 15,000-30,000 years ago. One possible reason is that many thousands of years ago humans lived in a world of dangerous predators ⓑ <u>which</u> they had to have their wits about them at all times to avoid ⓒ <u>being killed</u>. Today, we have effectively domesticated ourselves and many of the tasks of survival — from avoiding immediate death to building shelters to ⓓ <u>obtain</u> food — have been outsourced to the wider society. We are smaller than our ancestors too, and it is a characteristic of domestic animals ⓔ <u>what</u> they are generally smaller than their wild cousins. None of this may mean we are dumber — brain size is not necessarily an indicator of human intelligence — but it may mean that our brains today are wired up ⓕ <u>different</u>, and perhaps more efficiently, than those of our ancestors.

① 1개　② 2개　③ 3개　④ 4개　⑤ 5개

ⓐ: ＿＿＿＿＿＿ → ＿＿＿＿＿＿

ⓑ: ＿＿＿＿＿＿ → ＿＿＿＿＿＿

ⓒ: ＿＿＿＿＿＿ → ＿＿＿＿＿＿

ⓓ: ＿＿＿＿＿＿ → ＿＿＿＿＿＿

ⓔ: ＿＿＿＿＿＿ → ＿＿＿＿＿＿

ⓕ: ＿＿＿＿＿＿ → ＿＿＿＿＿＿

2022년_고1_9월_인천광역시 교육청_학력평가_30번

11. 밑줄 친 부분 중, 어법상 틀린 개수를 고르고 틀린 부분은 올바르게 고치시오.319)

It is widely believed ⓐ <u>that</u> certain herbs somehow magically improve the work of certain organs, and "cure" specific diseases as a result. Such statements are unscientific and groundless. Sometimes herbs ⓑ <u>appear</u> to work, since they tend to increase your blood circulation in an aggressive attempt by your body to eliminate them from your system. That can create a temporary feeling of a high, ⓒ <u>that</u> makes it seem as if your health condition has improved. Also, herbs can have a placebo effect, just like any other method, thus helping you feel better. Whatever the case, it is your body that has the intelligence to regain health, and not the herbs. How can herbs have the intelligence ⓓ <u>needing</u> to direct your body into getting healthier? That is impossible. ⓔ <u>Try</u> to imagine how herbs might come into your body and intelligently fix your problems. If you try to do that, you will see how impossible it seems. Otherwise, it would mean that herbs are more intelligent than the human body, ⓕ <u>which</u> is truly hard to believe.

*placebo effect: 위약 효과

① 1개   ② 2개   ③ 3개   ④ 4개   ⑤ 5개

ⓐ: _____ → _____

ⓑ: _____ → _____

ⓒ: _____ → _____

ⓓ: _____ → _____

ⓔ: _____ → _____

ⓕ: _____ → _____

2022년_고1_9월_인천광역시 교육청_학력평가_31번

12. 밑줄 친 부분 중, 어법상 틀린 개수를 고르고 틀린 부분은 올바르게 고치시오.320)

We worry that the robots are ⓐ <u>taking</u> our jobs, but just as common a problem is that the robots are taking our judgment. In the large warehouses so common behind the scenes of today's economy, human 'pickers' hurry around grabbing products off shelves and ⓑ <u>moving</u> them to where they can be packed and ⓒ <u>dispatching</u>. In their ears are headpieces: the voice of 'Jennifer', a piece of software, ⓓ <u>telling</u> them where to go and what to do, controlling the smallest details of their movements. Jennifer breaks down instructions into tiny chunks, to minimise error and maximise productivity — for example, rather than picking eighteen copies of a book off a shelf, the human worker would be politely ⓔ <u>instructed</u> to pick five. Then another five. Then yet another five. Then another three. Working in such conditions reduces people to machines made of flesh. Rather than asking us to think or adapt, the Jennifer unit takes over the thought process and ⓕ <u>treating</u> workers as an inexpensive source of some visual processing and a pair of opposable thumbs.

*dispatch: 발송하다 **chunk: 덩어리

① 1개   ② 2개   ③ 3개   ④ 4개   ⑤ 5개

ⓐ: _____ → _____

ⓑ: _____ → _____

ⓒ: _____ → _____

ⓓ: _____ → _____

ⓔ: _____ → _____

ⓕ: _____ → _____

13. 밑줄 친 부분 중, 어법상 틀린 개수를 고르고 틀린 부분은 올바르게 고치시오.321)

The prevailing view among developmental scientists ⓐ <u>are</u> that people are active contributors to their own development. People are influenced by the physical and social contexts ⓑ <u>which</u> they live, but they also play a role in influencing their development by interacting with, and changing, those contexts. Even infants ⓒ <u>influence</u> the world around them and construct their own development through their interactions. Consider an infant who smiles at each ⓓ <u>adult</u> he sees; he influences his world because adults are likely to smile, use "baby talk," and play with him in response. The infant brings adults into close contact, ⓔ <u>makes</u> one-on-one interactions and creating opportunities for learning. By engaging the world around them, thinking, being curious, and ⓕ <u>interacting</u> with people, objects, and the world around them, individuals of all ages are "manufacturers of their own development."

① 1개　② 2개　③ 3개　④ 4개　⑤ 5개

ⓐ: ＿＿＿＿＿＿＿ → ＿＿＿＿＿＿＿

ⓑ: ＿＿＿＿＿＿＿ → ＿＿＿＿＿＿＿

ⓒ: ＿＿＿＿＿＿＿ → ＿＿＿＿＿＿＿

ⓓ: ＿＿＿＿＿＿＿ → ＿＿＿＿＿＿＿

ⓔ: ＿＿＿＿＿＿＿ → ＿＿＿＿＿＿＿

ⓕ: ＿＿＿＿＿＿＿ → ＿＿＿＿＿＿＿

14. 밑줄 친 부분 중, 어법상 틀린 개수를 고르고 틀린 부분은 올바르게 고치시오.322)

The demand for freshness can have hidden environmental costs. ⓐ <u>While</u> freshness is now being used as a term in food marketing as part of a return to nature, the demand for year-round supplies of fresh produce such as soft fruit and exotic vegetables has ⓑ <u>led</u> to the widespread use of hot houses in cold climates and increasing reliance on total quality control — management by temperature control, use of pesticides and computer/satellite-based logistics. The demand for freshness has also ⓒ <u>been contributed</u> to concerns about food wastage. Use of 'best before', 'sell by' and 'eat by' labels has ⓓ <u>legally</u> allowed institutional waste. Campaigners have ⓔ <u>exposed</u> the scandal of overproduction and waste. Tristram Stuart, one of the global band of anti-waste campaigners, argues that, with freshly made sandwiches, over-ordering is standard practice across the retail sector to avoid the appearance of empty shelf space, ⓕ <u>leads</u> to high volumes of waste when supply regularly exceeds demand.

* pesticide: 살충제 ** logistics: 물류, 유통

① 1개　② 2개　③ 3개　④ 4개　⑤ 5개

ⓐ: ＿＿＿＿＿＿＿ → ＿＿＿＿＿＿＿

ⓑ: ＿＿＿＿＿＿＿ → ＿＿＿＿＿＿＿

ⓒ: ＿＿＿＿＿＿＿ → ＿＿＿＿＿＿＿

ⓓ: ＿＿＿＿＿＿＿ → ＿＿＿＿＿＿＿

ⓔ: ＿＿＿＿＿＿＿ → ＿＿＿＿＿＿＿

ⓕ: ＿＿＿＿＿＿＿ → ＿＿＿＿＿＿＿

15. 밑줄 친 부분 중, 어법상 틀린 개수를 고르고 틀린 부분은 올바르게 고치시오.323)

In the studies of Colin Cherry at the Massachusetts Institute for Technology back in the 1950s, his participants listened to voices in one ear at a time and then through both ears in an effort to determine ⓐ whether we can listen to two people talk at the same time. One ear always ⓑ contained a message that the listener had to repeat back (called "shadowing") while ⓒ the other ear included people speaking. The trick was to ⓓ see if you could totally focus on the main message and also hear someone talking in your other ear. Cleverly, Cherry found it was impossible ⓔ of his participants to know whether the message in the other ear was spoken by a man or woman, in English or another language, or was even ⓕ comprising of real words at all! In other words, people could not process two pieces of information at the same time.

① 1개   ② 2개   ③ 3개   ④ 4개   ⑤ 5개

ⓐ: _____ → _____

ⓑ: _____ → _____

ⓒ: _____ → _____

ⓓ: _____ → _____

ⓔ: _____ → _____

ⓕ: _____ → _____

16. 밑줄 친 부분 중, 어법상 틀린 개수를 고르고 틀린 부분은 올바르게 고치시오.324)

The fast-paced evolution of Information and Communication Technologies (ICTs) has ⓐ radically transformed the dynamics and business models of the tourism and hospitality industry. This leads to new levels/forms of competitiveness among service providers and ⓑ transforms the customer experience through new services. Creating unique experiences and providing convenient services to customers ⓒ lead to satisfaction and, eventually, customer loyalty to the service provider or brand (i.e., hotels). In particular, the most recent technological boost ⓓ receiving by the tourism sector ⓔ being represented by mobile applications. Indeed, ⓕ empowering tourists with mobile access to services such as hotel reservations, airline ticketing, and recommendations for local attractions generates strong interest and considerable profits.

* hospitality industry: 서비스업(호텔·식당업 등)

① 1개   ② 2개   ③ 3개   ④ 4개   ⑤ 5개

ⓐ: _____ → _____

ⓑ: _____ → _____

ⓒ: _____ → _____

ⓓ: _____ → _____

ⓔ: _____ → _____

ⓕ: _____ → _____

2022년_고1_9월_인천광역시 교육청_학력평가_36번

17. 밑줄 친 부분 중, 어법상 틀린 개수를 고르고 틀린 부분은 올바르게 고치시오.325)

With ⓐ <u>nearly</u> a billion hungry people in the world, there is obviously no single cause. However, far and away the biggest cause is poverty. Seventy-nine percent of the world's hungry ⓑ <u>lives</u> in nations that are net exporters of food. How can this be? The reason people are hungry in those countries ⓒ <u>is</u> that the products produced there can be sold on the world market for more than the local citizens can afford to ⓓ <u>paying</u> for them. In the modern age you do not starve because you have no food, you starve ⓔ <u>because</u> you have no money. So the problem really is that food is, in the grand scheme of things, too expensive and many people are ⓕ <u>so</u> poor to buy it. The answer will be in continuing the trend of lowering the cost of food.

* net exporter: 순 수출국 ** scheme: 체계, 조직

① 1개　② 2개　③ 3개　④ 4개　⑤ 5개

ⓐ: ＿＿＿＿＿＿＿ → ＿＿＿＿＿＿＿

ⓑ: ＿＿＿＿＿＿＿ → ＿＿＿＿＿＿＿

ⓒ: ＿＿＿＿＿＿＿ → ＿＿＿＿＿＿＿

ⓓ: ＿＿＿＿＿＿＿ → ＿＿＿＿＿＿＿

ⓔ: ＿＿＿＿＿＿＿ → ＿＿＿＿＿＿＿

ⓕ: ＿＿＿＿＿＿＿ → ＿＿＿＿＿＿＿

2022년_고1_9월_인천광역시 교육청_학력평가_37번

18. 밑줄 친 부분 중, 어법상 틀린 개수를 고르고 틀린 부분은 올바르게 고치시오.326)

Most people have a perfect time of day when they feel they are at their best, whether in the morning, evening, or afternoon. Some of us are night owls, some early birds, and ⓐ <u>others</u> in between may feel most active during the afternoon hours. If you are able to organize your day and divide your work, ⓑ <u>making</u> it a point to deal with tasks that demand attention at your best time of the day. However, if the task you face ⓒ <u>demands</u> creativity and novel ideas, it's best to tackle it at your "worst" time of day! So if you are an early bird, make sure ⓓ <u>to attack</u> your creative task in the evening, and vice versa for night owls. When your mind and body are less alert than at your "peak" hours, the muse of creativity awakens and is ⓔ <u>allowing</u> to roam more freely. In other words, when your mental machinery is loose rather than standing at attention, the creativity ⓕ <u>is flowed</u>.

*roam: (어슬렁어슬렁) 거닐다

① 1개　② 2개　③ 3개　④ 4개　⑤ 5개

ⓐ: ＿＿＿＿＿＿＿ → ＿＿＿＿＿＿＿

ⓑ: ＿＿＿＿＿＿＿ → ＿＿＿＿＿＿＿

ⓒ: ＿＿＿＿＿＿＿ → ＿＿＿＿＿＿＿

ⓓ: ＿＿＿＿＿＿＿ → ＿＿＿＿＿＿＿

ⓔ: ＿＿＿＿＿＿＿ → ＿＿＿＿＿＿＿

ⓕ: ＿＿＿＿＿＿＿ → ＿＿＿＿＿＿＿

2022년_고1_9월_인천광역시 교육청_학력평가_38번

19. 밑줄 친 부분 중, 어법상 틀린 개수를 고르고 틀린 부분은 올바르게 고치시오.327)

Television is the number one leisure activity in the United States and Europe, ⓐ <u>consumed</u> more than half of our free time. We generally think of television as a way to relax, tune out, and escape from our troubles for a bit each day. ⓑ <u>While</u> this is true, there is increasing evidence that we are more ⓒ <u>motivating</u> to tune in to our favorite shows and characters when we are feeling lonely or have a greater need for social connection. Television watching does ⓓ <u>satisfy</u> these social needs to some extent, at least in the short run. Unfortunately, it is also likely to "crowd out" other activities that ⓔ <u>are produced</u> more sustainable social contributions to our social well-being. The more television we watch, the less likely we are to volunteer our time or to spend time with people in our social networks. In other words, the more time we make for Friends, ⓕ <u>a</u> less time we have for friends in real life.

*Friends: 프렌즈(미국의 한 방송국에서 방영된 시트콤)

① 1개 ② 2개 ③ 3개 ④ 4개 ⑤ 5개

ⓐ: _____ → _____

ⓑ: _____ → _____

ⓒ: _____ → _____

ⓓ: _____ → _____

ⓔ: _____ → _____

ⓕ: _____ → _____

2022년_고1_9월_인천광역시 교육청_학력평가_39번

20. 밑줄 친 부분 중, 어법상 틀린 개수를 고르고 틀린 부분은 올바르게 고치시오.328)

We often associate the concept of temperature with how hot or cold an object ⓐ <u>feels</u> when we touch it. In this way, our senses ⓑ <u>provide</u> us with a qualitative indication of temperature. Our senses, however, are unreliable and often mislead us. For example, if you stand in bare feet with one foot on carpet and the other on a tile floor, the tile feels colder than the carpet ⓒ <u>despite</u> both are at the same temperature. The two objects feel different because tile transfers energy by heat at a higher rate than carpet ⓓ <u>is</u>. Your skin "measures" the rate of energy transfer by heat rather than the actual temperature. ⓔ <u>That</u> we need is a reliable and reproducible method for measuring the relative hotness or coldness of objects rather than the rate of energy transfer. Scientists have ⓕ <u>been developed</u> a variety of thermometers for making such quantitative measurements.

*thermometer: 온도계

① 1개 ② 2개 ③ 3개 ④ 4개 ⑤ 5개

ⓐ: _____ → _____

ⓑ: _____ → _____

ⓒ: _____ → _____

ⓓ: _____ → _____

ⓔ: _____ → _____

ⓕ: _____ → _____

2022년_고1_9월_인천광역시 교육청_학력평가_40번

21. 밑줄 친 부분 중, 어법상 틀린 개수를 고르고 틀린 부분은 올바르게 고치시오.329)

My colleagues and I ran an experiment testing two different messages ⓐ <u>meant</u> to convince thousands of resistant alumni to make a donation. One message emphasized the opportunity to do good: donating would benefit students, faculty, and staff. The other emphasized the opportunity to feel good: donors would enjoy the warm glow of giving. The two messages were equally effective: in both cases, 6.5 percent of the unwilling alumni ended up ⓑ <u>to donate</u>. Then we combined them, because two reasons are better than one. Except they ⓒ <u>weren't</u>. When we put the two reasons together, the giving rate dropped below 3 percent. Each reason alone was more than twice as ⓓ <u>effectively</u> as the two combined. The audience was already skeptical. When we gave them different kinds of reasons to donate, we triggered their awareness that someone was trying to persuade ⓔ <u>themselves</u> — and they shielded themselves against it.

* alumni: 졸업생 ** skeptical: 회의적인

↓

In the experiment mentioned above, when the two different reasons to donate were given simultaneously, the audience was less likely to be ⓕ <u>convincing</u> because they could recognize the intention to persuade them.

① 1개 ② 2개 ③ 3개 ④ 4개 ⑤ 5개

ⓐ: _____ → _____

ⓑ: _____ → _____

ⓒ: _____ → _____

ⓓ: _____ → _____

ⓔ: _____ → _____

ⓕ: _____ → _____

2022년_고1_9월_인천광역시 교육청_학력평가_41~42번

22. 밑줄 친 부분 중, 어법상 틀린 개수를 고르고 틀린 부분은 올바르게 고치시오.330)

In a society ⓐ <u>that</u> rejects the consumption of insects there are some individuals who overcome this rejection, but most will continue with this attitude. It may be very difficult to convince an entire society that insects are totally suitable for consumption. However, there are examples ⓑ <u>which</u> this reversal of attitudes about certain foods has happened to an entire society. Several examples in the past 120 years from European-American society are: considering lobster a luxury food instead of a food for servants and prisoners; considering sushi a safe and delicious food; and considering pizza not just a food for the rural poor of Sicily. In Latin American countries, where insects are already ⓒ <u>consumed</u>, a portion of the population hates their consumption and ⓓ <u>associate</u> it with poverty. There are also examples of people who have had the habit of consuming them and abandoned that habit ⓔ <u>because</u> shame, and because they do not want to be categorized as poor or uncivilized. According to Esther Katz, an anthropologist, if the consumption of insects as a food luxury is to be promoted, there would be more chances that some individuals who do not present this habit overcome ideas ⓕ <u>under which</u> they were educated. And this could also help to revalue the consumption of insects by those people who already eat them.

① 1개 ② 2개 ③ 3개 ④ 4개 ⑤ 5개

ⓐ: _____ → _____

ⓑ: _____ → _____

ⓒ: _____ → _____

ⓓ: _____ → _____

ⓔ: _____ → _____

ⓕ: _____ → _____

어법 Lv_심화1(주관식)

2022년_고1_9월_인천광역시 교육청_학력평가_18번

1. 다음 글의 밑줄 친 ①~⑤ 중, 어법상 틀린 문장을 찾고 틀린 부분을 찾은 뒤, 올바른 문장으로 수정하시오.331)

Dear Parents/Guardians, Class parties ①**will hold on the afternoon December 16th, 2022**. Children may bring in sweets, crisps, biscuits, cakes, and drinks. ② **We are requesting that** children do not bring in home-cooked or prepared food. All food should arrive in a sealed packet ③**with the ingredients clear listing**. Fruit and vegetables are welcomed ④**if they are pre-packed in a sealed packet from the shop**. Please DO NOT send any food into school containing nuts ⑤**due to we have many children with severe nut allergies**. Please check the ingredients of all food your children bring carefully. Thank you for your continued support and cooperation.
Yours sincerely, Lisa Brown, Headteacher

번호	틀린 부분
( )	틀린부분 [ ]
	↓
	수정문장
( )	틀린부분 [ ]
	↓
	수정문장
( )	틀린부분 [ ]
	↓
	수정문장

2022년_고1_9월_인천광역시 교육청_학력평가_19번

2. 다음 글의 밑줄 친 ①~⑤ 중, 어법상 틀린 문장을 찾고 틀린 부분을 찾은 뒤, 올바른 문장으로 수정하시오.332)

It was two hours before the submission deadline and ①**I still didn't finished my news article.** I sat at the desk, but suddenly, the typewriter didn't work. ②**No matter how I tapped hard the keys**, the levers wouldn't move to strike the paper. I started to realize ③**that I would not be able to finish the article on time**. Desperately, I rested the typewriter on my lap and started hitting each key with ④**due to force as I could be managed**. Nothing happened. Thinking something might have happened inside of it, I opened the cover, lifted up the keys, and found the problem — a paper clip. The keys had no room to move. ⑤**After picking it out**, I pressed and pulled some parts. The keys moved smoothly again. I breathed deeply and smiled. Now I knew that I could finish my article on time.

번호	틀린 부분
( )	틀린부분 [ ]
	↓
	수정문장
( )	틀린부분 [ ]
	↓
	수정문장
( )	틀린부분 [ ]
	↓
	수정문장

3. 다음 글의 밑줄 친 ①~⑤ 중, 어법상 틀린 문장을 찾고 틀린 부분을 찾은 뒤, 올바른 문장으로 수정하시오. 333)

Experts on writing say, "Get rid of as many words as possible." ①**Each word must do important something.** If it doesn't, get rid of it. Well, this doesn't work for speaking. It takes more words to introduce, express, ②**and adequately elaborates an idea in speech** than it takes in writing. Why is this so? While the reader can reread, the listener cannot rehear. ③**Speakers do not come equipped with a replay button**. Because listeners are easily distracted, ④**they will miss many pieces of which a speaker says**. If they miss the crucial sentence, they may never catch up. This makes it necessary for speakers to talk longer about their points, ⑤**using more words on them than would be used to express the same idea in writing**.

번호	틀린 부분	
( )	틀린부분 [	]
	↓	
	수정문장	
( )	틀린부분 [	]
	↓	
	수정문장	
( )	틀린부분 [	]
	↓	
	수정문장	

4. 다음 글의 밑줄 친 ①~⑤ 중, 어법상 틀린 문장을 찾고 틀린 부분을 찾은 뒤, 올바른 문장으로 수정하시오. 334)

Is the customer always right? When customers return a broken product to a famous company, ①**which makes kitchen and bathroom fixtures**, the company nearly always offers a replacement to maintain good customer relations. Still, "there are times you've got to say 'no,'" explains the warranty expert of the company, ②**such as when a product is undamaged or has abused**. Entrepreneur Lauren Thorp, who owns an e-commerce company, says, "While the customer is 'always' right, ③**sometimes you just have to fire a customer**." ④**When Thorp has tried everything resolving a complaint and realizes** that the customer will be dissatisfied no matter what, she returns her attention to the rest of her customers, ⑤**who she says is "the reason for my success."**

번호	틀린 부분	
( )	틀린부분 [	]
	↓	
	수정문장	
( )	틀린부분 [	]
	↓	
	수정문장	
( )	틀린부분 [	]
	↓	
	수정문장	

2022년_고1_9월_인천광역시 교육청_학력평가_22번

5. 다음 글의 밑줄 친 ①~⑤ 중, 어법상 틀린 문장을 찾고 틀린 부분을 찾은 뒤, 올바른 문장으로 수정하시오.335)

A recent study from Carnegie Mellon University in Pittsburgh, called "When Too Much of a Good Thing May Be Bad," indicates that classrooms ①<u>with too much decoration being a source of distraction for young children</u> and directly affect their cognitive performance. ②<u>Being visually overstimulated</u>, ③<u>the children have a great deal of difficulty concentrated and end up with worse academic results</u>. On the other hand, if there is not much decoration on the classroom walls, ④<u>the children are less distracted, spend more time on their activities, and learn more</u>. So it's our job, ⑤<u>in order to supporting their attention</u>, to find the right balance between excessive decoration and the complete absence of it.

번호	틀린 부분	
( )	틀린부분 [	]
	↓	
	수정문장	
( )	틀린부분 [	]
	↓	
	수정문장	
( )	틀린부분 [	]
	↓	
	수정문장	

2022년_고1_9월_인천광역시 교육청_학력평가_23번

6. 다음 글의 밑줄 친 ①~⑤ 중, 어법상 틀린 문장을 찾고 틀린 부분을 찾은 뒤, 올바른 문장으로 수정하시오.336)

For creatures like us, evolution smiled upon those ①<u>with a strong needed to belong</u>. Survival and reproduction are the criteria of success by natural selection, ②<u>and formed relationships with other people can be useful for both survival and reproduction</u>. Groups can share resources, care for sick members, scare off predators, fight together against enemies, divide tasks ③<u>so as to improve efficiency</u>, and contribute to survival in many other ways. In particular, ④<u>if an individual and a group want the same resource</u>, the group will generally prevail, so competition for resources would especially favor a need to belong. Belongingness will likewise promote reproduction, such as by bringing potential mates into contact with each other, and in particular by keeping parents together to care for their children, ⑤<u>who are much more likely to surviving if they have more than one caregiver</u>.

번호	틀린 부분	
( )	틀린부분 [	]
	↓	
	수정문장	
( )	틀린부분 [	]
	↓	
	수정문장	
( )	틀린부분 [	]
	↓	
	수정문장	

7. 다음 글의 밑줄 친 ①~⑤ 중, 어법상 틀린 문장을 찾고 틀린 부분을 찾은 뒤, 올바른 문장으로 수정하시오.337)

Many people make a mistake of only operating along the safe zones, and in the process they miss the opportunity to achieve greater things. ①**They are so** ②**because of a fear of the unknown and a fear of treading the unknown paths of life**. Those that are ③**brave** enough ③**to take those roads less travelling** are able to get great returns and ④**derive major satisfaction out of their courageous moves**. Being overcautious will mean that ⑤**you will miss to attain the greatest levels of your potential**. You must learn to take those chances that many people around you will not take, because your success will flow from those bold decisions that you will take along the way.

번호	틀린 부분
( )	틀린부분 [ ]
	↓
	수정문장
( )	틀린부분 [ ]
	↓
	수정문장
( )	틀린부분 [ ]
	↓
	수정문장

8. 다음 글의 밑줄 친 ①~⑤ 중, 어법상 틀린 문장을 찾고 틀린 부분을 찾은 뒤, 올바른 문장으로 수정하시오.338)

The graph above shows the share of the urban population by continent in 1950 and in 2020. For each continent, the share of the urban population in 2020 was ①**larger than that in 1950**. From 1950 to 2020, ②**the share of the urban population in Africa increasing from 14.3% to 43.5%**. The share of the urban population in Asia was ③**the second lowest in 1950 but not in 2020**. In 1950, the share of the urban population in Europe was ④**larger than it in Latin America** and the Caribbean, whereas the reverse was true in 2020. Among the five continents, ⑤**Northern America was ranking in the first position for the share of the urban population in both 1950 and 2020**.

번호	틀린 부분
( )	틀린부분 [ ]
	↓
	수정문장
( )	틀린부분 [ ]
	↓
	수정문장
( )	틀린부분 [ ]
	↓
	수정문장

2022년_고1_9월_인천광역시 교육청_학력평가_26번

9. 다음 글의 밑줄 친 ①~⑤ 중, 어법상 틀린 문장을 찾고 틀린 부분을 찾은 뒤, 올바른 문장으로 수정하시오.339)

Wilbur Smith was a South African novelist specialising in historical fiction. Smith wanted to become a journalist, ①**wrote about social conditions in South Africa**, but his father was never supportive of his writing and ②**forced him to get a real job**. Smith studied further and became a tax accountant, but he finally turned back to his love of writing. He wrote his first novel, ③**The Gods First Make Mad, and was received 20 rejections by 1962**. In 1964, Smith published another novel, When the Lion Feeds, and ④**it went on to being successful, selling around the world**. A famous actor and film producer bought the film rights for When the Lion Feeds, although no movie resulted. By the time of his death in 2021 ⑤**he had published 49 novels, selling more than 140 million copies worldwide**.

번호	틀린 부분	
( )	틀린부분 [	]
	↓	
	수정문장	
( )	틀린부분 [	]
	↓	
	수정문장	
( )	틀린부분 [	]
	↓	
	수정문장	

2022년_고1_9월_인천광역시 교육청_학력평가_27번

10. 다음 글의 밑줄 친 ①~⑤ 중, 어법상 틀린 문장을 찾고 틀린 부분을 찾은 뒤, 올바른 문장으로 수정하시오.340)

2022 Springfield Park Yoga Class
The popular yoga class in Springfield Park returns!
①**Enjoy yoga hosting on the park lawn**. ②**If you can't make it to the park**, join us online on our social media platforms!
◆When: Saturdays, 2 p.m. to 3 p.m., September
◆Registration: ③**At least TWO hours before each class will start**, sign up here.
◆Notes
•For online classes: find a quiet space ④**with enough room for you to stretch out**.
•For classes in the park: mats are not provided, so bring your own!
※⑤**The class will cancel** if the weather is unfavorable. For more information, click here.

번호	틀린 부분	
( )	틀린부분 [	]
	↓	
	수정문장	
( )	틀린부분 [	]
	↓	
	수정문장	
( )	틀린부분 [	]
	↓	
	수정문장	

2022년_고1_9월_인천광역시 교육청_학력평가_28번

11. 다음 글의 밑줄 친 ①~⑤ 중, 어법상 틀린 문장을 찾고 틀린 부분을 찾은 뒤, 올바른 문장으로 수정하시오.341)

Kenner High School's Water Challenge
Kenner High School's Water Challenge is ①a new contest to propose measures against water pollution. ②Please share your ideas for dealing with water pollution!
Submission
How: Submit your proposal by email to admin@khswater.edu.
When: September 5, 2022 to September 23, 2022
Details
③Participants must enter in teams of four and can only join with one team.
④Submission is limited to one proposal per teams.
⑤Participants must use the proposal form providing on the website.
Prizes
1st: $50 gift certificate
2nd: $30 gift certificate
3rd: $10 gift certificate
Please visit www.khswater.edu to learn more about the challenge.

번호	틀린 부분
( )	틀린부분 [ ]
	↓
	수정문장
( )	틀린부분 [ ]
	↓
	수정문장
( )	틀린부분 [ ]
	↓
	수정문장

2022년_고1_9월_인천광역시 교육청_학력평가_29번

12. 다음 글의 밑줄 친 ①~⑤ 중, 어법상 틀린 문장을 찾고 틀린 부분을 찾은 뒤, 올바른 문장으로 수정하시오.342)

The human brain, it turns out, has shrunk in mass by about 10 percent ①since it was peaked in size 15,000-30,000 years ago. One possible reason is that many thousands of years ago humans lived in a world of dangerous predators ②what they had to have their wits about them at all times to avoid to be killed. Today, we have effectively domesticated ourselves and many of the tasks of survival — ③ from avoiding immediate death to building shelters to obtaining food — have been outsourced to the wider society. We are smaller than our ancestors too, and it is a characteristic of domestic animals ④ which they are generally smaller than their wild cousins. None of this may mean we are dumber — brain size is not necessarily an indicator of human intelligence — but it may mean ⑤that our brains today are wired up differently, and perhaps more efficiently, than those of our ancestors.

번호	틀린 부분
( )	틀린부분 [ ]
	↓
	수정문장
( )	틀린부분 [ ]
	↓
	수정문장
( )	틀린부분 [ ]
	↓
	수정문장

2022년_고1_9월_인천광역시 교육청_학력평가_30번

13. 다음 글의 밑줄 친 ①~⑤ 중, 어법상 틀린 문장을 찾고 틀린 부분을 찾은 뒤, 올바른 문장으로 수정하시오.343)

It is widely believed that certain herbs somehow magically improve the work of certain organs, and "cure" specific diseases as a result. Such statements are unscientific and groundless. ①<u>Sometimes herbs are appeared to work</u>, since they tend to increase your blood circulation in an aggressive attempt by your body to eliminate them from your system. That can create a temporary feeling of a high, ②<u>which makes it seem as if your health condition has improved</u>. Also, herbs can have a placebo effect, just like any other method, thus helping you feel better. Whatever the case, ③<u>it is your body that has the intelligence to regain health, and not the herbs</u>. How can herbs have the intelligence needed to direct your body into getting healthier? That is impossible. ④<u>Try to imagine how herbs might be come into your body and intelligently fixing your problems</u>. If you try to do that, ⑤<u>you will see how it seems impossible</u>. Otherwise, it would mean that herbs are more intelligent than the human body, which is truly hard to believe.

*placebo effect: 위약 효과

번호	틀린 부분	
( )	틀린부분 [	]
	↓	
	수정문장	
( )	틀린부분 [	]
	↓	
	수정문장	
( )	틀린부분 [	]
	↓	
	수정문장	

2022년_고1_9월_인천광역시 교육청_학력평가_31번

14. 다음 글의 밑줄 친 ①~⑤ 중, 어법상 틀린 문장을 찾고 틀린 부분을 찾은 뒤, 올바른 문장으로 수정하시오.344)

①<u>We worry that the robots are taking our jobs</u>, but just as common a problem is that the robots are taking our judgment. In the large warehouses so common behind the scenes of today's economy, human 'pickers' hurry around grabbing products off shelves and ②<u>moving them to where they can be packed and dispatch</u>. In their ears are headpieces: the voice of 'Jennifer', a piece of software, tells them where to go and what to do, ③<u>controls the smallest details of their movements</u>. Jennifer breaks down instructions into tiny chunks, to minimise error and maximise productivity — for example, rather than picking eighteen copies of a book off a shelf, ④<u>the human worker would be politely instructing to pick five</u>. Then another five. Then yet another five. Then another three. ⑤<u>Working in such conditions reduces people to machines made of flesh</u>. Rather than asking us to think or adapt, the Jennifer unit takes over the thought process and treats workers as an inexpensive source of some visual processing and a pair of opposable thumbs.

*dispatch: 발송하다 **chunk: 덩어리

번호	틀린 부분	
( )	틀린부분 [	]
	↓	
	수정문장	
( )	틀린부분 [	]
	↓	
	수정문장	
( )	틀린부분 [	]
	↓	
	수정문장	

2022년_고1_9월_인천광역시 교육청_학력평가_32번

15. 다음 글의 밑줄 친 ①~⑤ 중, 어법상 틀린 문장을 찾고 틀린 부분을 찾은 뒤, 올바른 문장으로 수정하시오.345)

①<u>The prevailing view among developmental scientists is</u> that people are active contributors to their own development. People are influenced ②<u>by the physical and social contexts which they live</u>, but they also play a role in influencing their development by interacting with, and changing, those contexts. Even infants influence the world around them and construct their own development through their interactions. ③<u>Consider an infant who smiles at each adults he sees</u>; he influences his world ④<u>because adults are likely to smile</u>, use "baby talk," and play with him in response. The infant brings adults into close contact, ⑤<u>making one-on-one interactions and creates opportunities for learning</u>. By engaging the world around them, thinking, being curious, and interacting with people, objects, and the world around them, individuals of all ages are "manufacturers of their own development."

번호	틀린 부분
( )	틀린부분 [ ]
	↓
	수정문장
( )	틀린부분 [ ]
	↓
	수정문장
( )	틀린부분 [ ]
	↓
	수정문장

2022년_고1_9월_인천광역시 교육청_학력평가_33번

16. 다음 글의 밑줄 친 ①~⑤ 중, 어법상 틀린 문장을 찾고 틀린 부분을 찾은 뒤, 올바른 문장으로 수정하시오.346)

①<u>The demand for freshness can have hidden environmental costs</u>. While ②<u>freshness is now using as a term in food marketing as part of a return to nature</u>, the demand for year-round supplies of fresh produce such as soft fruit and exotic vegetables has led to the widespread use of hot houses in cold climates and increasing reliance on total quality control — management by temperature control, use of pesticides and computer/satellite-based logistics. ③<u>The demand for freshness has also contributed to concerns</u> about food wastage. Use of 'best before', 'sell by' and 'eat by' labels has legally allowed institutional waste. ④<u>Campaigners have been exposed the scandal of overproduction and waste</u>. Tristram Stuart, one of the global band of anti-waste campaigners, argues that, with freshly made sandwiches, over-ordering is standard practice across the retail sector to avoid the appearance of empty shelf space, ⑤<u>leads to high volumes of waste when supply regularly exceeds demand</u>.

* pesticide: 살충제 ** logistics: 물류, 유통

번호	틀린 부분
( )	틀린부분 [ ]
	↓
	수정문장
( )	틀린부분 [ ]
	↓
	수정문장
( )	틀린부분 [ ]
	↓
	수정문장

스승의날 영어연구소

2022년_고1_9월_인천광역시 교육청_학력평가_34번

17. 다음 글의 밑줄 친 ①~⑤ 중, 어법상 틀린 문장을 찾고 틀린 부분을 찾은 뒤, 올바른 문장으로 수정하시오.347)

In the studies of Colin Cherry at the Massachusetts Institute for Technology back in the 1950s, his participants listened to voices in one ear at a time and then through both ears in an effort to determine ①<u>what we can listen to two people talk at the same time</u>. ②<u>One ear always contained a message</u> that the listener had to repeat back (called "shadowing") ③<u>while the other ear including people speaking</u>. The trick was to see if you could totally focus on the main message and also hear someone talking in your other ear. Cleverly, ④<u>Cherry found them was impossible of his participants</u> to know whether ⑤<u>the message in the other ear was spoken by a man or woman</u>, in English or another language, or was even comprised of real words at all! In other words, people could not process two pieces of information at the same time.

번호	틀린 부분
( )	틀린부분 [ ]
	↓
	수정문장
( )	틀린부분 [ ]
	↓
	수정문장
( )	틀린부분 [ ]
	↓
	수정문장

2022년_고1_9월_인천광역시 교육청_학력평가_35번

18. 다음 글의 밑줄 친 ①~⑤ 중, 어법상 틀린 문장을 찾고 틀린 부분을 찾은 뒤, 올바른 문장으로 수정하시오.348)

①<u>The fast-paced evolution of Information and Communication Technologies (ICTs) has radically transformed the dynamics</u> and business models of the tourism and hospitality industry. This leads to new levels/forms of competitiveness among service providers and transforms the customer experience through new services. Creating unique experiences and providing convenient services to customers ② <u>leading to satisfaction and, eventually, customer loyalty to the service provider or brand</u> (i.e., hotels). In particular, ③<u>the most recent technological boost received by the tourism sector is represented by mobile applications</u>. Indeed, ④<u>being empowering tourists with mobile access to services</u> such as hotel reservations, airline ticketing, and ⑤<u>recommendations for local attractions generating strong interest and considerable profits</u>.

* hospitality industry: 서비스업(호텔·식당업 등)

번호	틀린 부분
( )	틀린부분 [ ]
	↓
	수정문장
( )	틀린부분 [ ]
	↓
	수정문장
( )	틀린부분 [ ]
	↓
	수정문장

2022년_고1_9월_인천광역시 교육청_학력평가_36번

19. 다음 글의 밑줄 친 ①~⑤ 중, 어법상 틀린 문장을 찾고 틀린 부분을 찾은 뒤, 올바른 문장으로 수정하시오.349)

With nearly a billion hungry people in the world, there is obviously no single cause. However, far and away the biggest cause is poverty. ①**Seventy-nine percent of the world's hungry live in nations** that are net exporters of food. How can this be? The reason people are hungry in those countries is ② **that the products produce there can be sold on the world market** ③**for more than the local citizens can afford to pay for them**. In the modern age you do not starve because you have no food, you starve because you have no money. ④**So the problem really is which food is**, in the grand scheme of things, ⑤**too expensive and many people are so poor buying it**. The answer will be in continuing the trend of lowering the cost of food.

* net exporter: 순 수출국 ** scheme: 체계, 조직

번호	틀린 부분	
( )	틀린부분 [	]
	↓	
	수정문장	
( )	틀린부분 [	]
	↓	
	수정문장	
( )	틀린부분 [	]
	↓	
	수정문장	

2022년_고1_9월_인천광역시 교육청_학력평가_37번

20. 다음 글의 밑줄 친 ①~⑤ 중, 어법상 틀린 문장을 찾고 틀린 부분을 찾은 뒤, 올바른 문장으로 수정하시오.350)

Most people have a perfect time of day ①**when they feel they being at their best**, whether in the morning, evening, or afternoon. Some of us are night owls, some early birds, and ②**others in between may feel most active during the afternoon hours**. If you are able to organize your day and divide your work, make it a point to deal with tasks that demand attention at your best time of the day. However, ③**if the task you face demanding creativity and novel ideas**, it's best to tackle it at your "worst" time of day! So if you are an early bird, ④**make sure to attack your creative task in the evening**, and vice versa for night owls. When your mind and body are less alert than at your "peak" hours, the muse of creativity awakens and is allowed to roam more freely. In other words, when your mental machinery is loose rather than standing at attention, ⑤**the creativity is flowed**.

*roam: (어슬렁어슬렁) 거닐다

번호	틀린 부분	
( )	틀린부분 [	]
	↓	
	수정문장	
( )	틀린부분 [	]
	↓	
	수정문장	
( )	틀린부분 [	]
	↓	
	수정문장	

2022년_고1_9월_인천광역시 교육청_학력평가_38번

21. 다음 글의 밑줄 친 ①~⑤ 중, 어법상 틀린 문장을 찾고 틀린 부분을 찾은 뒤, 올바른 문장으로 수정하시오.351)

Television is the number one leisure activity in the United States and Europe, ①consumes more than half of our free time. We generally think of television as a way to relax, tune out, and escape from our troubles for a bit each day. While this is true, there is increasing evidence ②that we are more motivated to tune in to our favorite shows and characters when we are feeling lonely or have a greater need for social connection. ③Television watching does satisfying these social needs to some extent, at least in the short run. Unfortunately, it is also likely to "crowd out" other activities ④that produce more sustainable social contributions to our social well-being. The more television we watch, the less likely we are to volunteer our time or ⑤ spending time with people in our social networks. In other words, the more time we make for Friends, the less time we have for friends in real life.

*Friends: 프렌즈(미국의 한 방송국에서 방영된 시트콤)

번호	틀린 부분	
( )	틀린부분 [	]
	↓	
	수정문장	
( )	틀린부분 [	]
	↓	
	수정문장	
( )	틀린부분 [	]
	↓	
	수정문장	

2022년_고1_9월_인천광역시 교육청_학력평가_39번

22. 다음 글의 밑줄 친 ①~⑤ 중, 어법상 틀린 문장을 찾고 틀린 부분을 찾은 뒤, 올바른 문장으로 수정하시오.352)

We often associate the concept of temperature ① with how hot or cold feels an object when we touch it. In this way, our senses provide us with a qualitative indication of temperature. Our senses, however, are unreliable and often mislead us. For example, if you stand in bare feet with one foot on carpet and the other on a tile floor, the tile feels colder than the carpet ②even though both are at the same temperature. The two objects feel different ③because tile transfers energy by heat at a higher rate than carpet is. Your skin "measures" the rate of energy transfer by heat rather than the actual temperature. ④What we need is a reliable and reproducible method for measuring the relative hotness or coldness of objects rather than the rate of energy transfer. ⑤Scientists have been developed a variety of thermometers for making such quantitative measurements.

*thermometer: 온도계

번호	틀린 부분	
( )	틀린부분 [	]
	↓	
	수정문장	
( )	틀린부분 [	]
	↓	
	수정문장	
( )	틀린부분 [	]
	↓	
	수정문장	

2022년_고1_9월_인천광역시 교육청_학력평가_40번

23. 다음 글의 밑줄 친 ①~⑤ 중, 어법상 틀린 문장을 찾고 틀린 부분을 찾은 뒤, 올바른 문장으로 수정하시오.353)

My colleagues and I ran an experiment testing two different messages ①meaning to convince thousands of resistant alumni making a donation. One message emphasized the opportunity to do good: donating would benefit students, faculty, and staff. The other emphasized the opportunity to feel good: donors would enjoy the warm glow of giving. The two messages were equally effective: in both cases, ②6.5 percent of the unwilling alumni ended up donated. Then we combined them, because two reasons are better than one. ③Except they weren't. When we put the two reasons together, the giving rate dropped below 3 percent. ④Each reason alone was more than twice as effectively as the two combined. The audience was already skeptical. When we gave them different kinds of reasons to donate, we triggered their awareness that someone was trying to persuade them — ⑤and they shielded themselves against it.

* alumni: 졸업생 ** skeptical: 회의적인

⬇

In the experiment mentioned above, when the two different reasons to donate were given simultaneously, the audience was less likely to be convinced because they could recognize the intention to persuade them.

번호	틀린 부분
( )	틀린부분 [ ]
	↓
	수정문장
( )	틀린부분 [ ]
	↓
	수정문장
( )	틀린부분 [ ]
	↓
	수정문장

2022년_고1_9월_인천광역시 교육청_학력평가_41~42번

24. 다음 글의 밑줄 친 ①~⑤ 중, 어법상 틀린 문장을 찾고 틀린 부분을 찾은 뒤, 올바른 문장으로 수정하시오.354)

In a society that rejects the consumption of insects there are some individuals who overcome this rejection, but most will continue with this attitude. It may be very difficult to convince an entire society ①that insects are totally suitable for consumption. However, ②there are examples in which this reversal of attitudes about certain foods has happened to an entire society. ③Several examples in the past 120 years from European-American society being: considering lobster a luxury food instead of a food for servants and prisoners; considering sushi a safe and delicious food; and considering pizza not just a food for the rural poor of Sicily. In Latin American countries, where insects are already consumed, ④a portion of the population hate their consumption and associate it with poverty. There are also examples of people who have had the habit of consuming them and abandoned that habit due to shame, and because they do not want to be categorized as poor or uncivilized. According to Esther Katz, an anthropologist, if the consumption of insects as a food luxury is to be promoted, there would be more chances that ⑤some individuals who do not present this habit overcoming ideas which they were educated. And this could also help to revalue the consumption of insects by those people who already eat them.

번호	틀린 부분
( )	틀린부분 [ ]
	↓
	수정문장
( )	틀린부분 [ ]
	↓
	수정문장
( )	틀린부분 [ ]
	↓
	수정문장

어법 Lv_심화2(주관식)

2022년_고1_9월_인천광역시 교육청_학력평가_18번

1. 다음 글에서 어법상 틀린 부분 5곳을 찾은 뒤, 수정하시오.355)

Dear Parents/Guardians, Class parties will hold on the afternoon December 16th, 2022. Children may bring in sweets, crisps, biscuits, cakes, and drinks. We are requested that children do not bring in home-cooked or prepared food. All food should arrive in a sealed packet with the ingredients clear listed. Fruit and vegetables are welcomed if they are pre-packed in a sealed packet from the shop. Please DO NOT send any food into school contained nuts due to we have many children with severe nut allergies. Please check the ingredients of all food your children bring careful. Thank you for your continued support and cooperation. Yours sincerely, Lisa Brown, Headteacher

①
틀린부분 [   ]
↓
수정부분 [   ]

②
틀린부분 [   ]
↓
수정부분 [   ]

③
틀린부분 [   ]
↓
수정부분 [   ]

④
틀린부분 [   ]
↓
수정부분 [   ]

⑤
틀린부분 [   ]
↓
수정부분 [   ]

2022년_고1_9월_인천광역시 교육청_학력평가_19번

2. 다음 글에서 어법상 틀린 부분 5곳을 찾은 뒤, 수정하시오.356)

It was two hours before the submission deadline and I still haven't finished my news article. I sat at the desk, but suddenly, the typewriter didn't work. No matter how I tapped hard the keys, the levers wouldn't move to strike the paper. I started to realize which I would not be able to finish the article on time. Desperately, I rested the typewriter on my lap and started hitting each key with as much force as I could be managed. Nothing happened. Thinking something might have happened inside of it, I opened the cover, lifted up the keys, and found the problem — a paper clip. The keys had no room to move. After picked it out, I pressed and pulled some parts. The keys moved smoothly again. I breathed deeply and smiled. Now I knew that I could finish my article on time.

①
틀린부분 [   ]
↓
수정부분 [   ]

②
틀린부분 [   ]
↓
수정부분 [   ]

③
틀린부분 [   ]
↓
수정부분 [   ]

④
틀린부분 [   ]
↓
수정부분 [   ]

⑤
틀린부분 [   ]
↓
수정부분 [   ]

2022년_고1_9월_인천광역시 교육청_학력평가_20번

3. 다음 글에서 어법상 틀린 부분 5곳을 찾은 뒤, 수정하시오.357)

Experts on writing say, "Get rid of as many words as possibly." Each words must do something important. If it doesn't, get rid of it. Well, this doesn't work for speaking. It takes more words to introduce, express, and adequately elaborates an idea in speech than it takes in writing. Why is this so? While the reader can reread, the listener cannot rehear. Speakers do not come equip with a replay button. Because listeners are easily distracted, they will miss many pieces of that a speaker says. If they miss the crucial sentence, they may never catch up. This makes it necessary for speakers to talk longer about their points, using more words on them than would be used to express the same idea in writing.

①	
틀린부분 [	]
↓	
수정부분 [	]
②	
틀린부분 [	]
↓	
수정부분 [	]
③	
틀린부분 [	]
↓	
수정부분 [	]
④	
틀린부분 [	]
↓	
수정부분 [	]
⑤	
틀린부분 [	]
↓	
수정부분 [	]

2022년_고1_9월_인천광역시 교육청_학력평가_21번

4. 다음 글에서 어법상 틀린 부분 5곳을 찾은 뒤, 수정하시오.358)

Is the customer always right? When customers return a broken product to a famous company, what makes kitchen and bathroom fixtures, the company nearly always offers a replacement to maintain good customer relations. Still, "there are times you've got to say 'no,'" explains the warranty expert of the company, such as when a product is undamaged or has abused. Entrepreneur Lauren Thorp, who owns an e-commerce company, says, "While the customer is 'always' right, sometimes you just have to fire a customer." When Thorp has been tried everything to resolve a complaint and realizes that the customer will be dissatisfying no matter what, she returns her attention to the rest of her customers, who she says is "the reason for my success."

①	
틀린부분 [	]
↓	
수정부분 [	]
②	
틀린부분 [	]
↓	
수정부분 [	]
③	
틀린부분 [	]
↓	
수정부분 [	]
④	
틀린부분 [	]
↓	
수정부분 [	]
⑤	
틀린부분 [	]
↓	
수정부분 [	]

5. 다음 글에서 어법상 틀린 부분 5곳을 찾은 뒤, 수정하시오.359)

A recent study from Carnegie Mellon University in Pittsburgh, called "When Too Much of a Good Thing May Be Bad," indicates that classrooms with too much decoration is a source of distraction for young children and directly affect their cognitive performance. Being visually overstimulating, the children have a great deal of difficulty concentrate and end up with worse academic results. On the other hand, if there is not much decoration on the classroom walls, the children are less distracting, spend more time on their activities, and learn more. So it's our job, in order to supporting their attention, to find the right balance between excessive decoration and the complete absence of it.

①
틀린부분 [   ]
↓
수정부분 [   ]
②
틀린부분 [   ]
↓
수정부분 [   ]
③
틀린부분 [   ]
↓
수정부분 [   ]
④
틀린부분 [   ]
↓
수정부분 [   ]
⑤
틀린부분 [   ]
↓
수정부분 [   ]

6. 다음 글에서 어법상 틀린 부분 5곳을 찾은 뒤, 수정하시오.360)

For creatures like us, evolution smiled upon those with a strong needed to belong. Survival and reproduction being the criteria of success by natural selection, and formed relationships with other people can be useful for both survival and reproduction. Groups can share resources, care for sick members, scare off predators, fight together against enemies, divide tasks so as for improving efficiency, and contribute to survival in many other ways. In particular, if an individual and a group wants the same resource, the group will generally prevail, so competition for resources would especially favor a need to belong. Belongingness will likewise promote reproduction, such as by bringing potential mates into contact with each other, and in particular by keeping parents together to care for their children, who are much more likely to survive if they have more than one caregiver.

①
틀린부분 [   ]
↓
수정부분 [   ]
②
틀린부분 [   ]
↓
수정부분 [   ]
③
틀린부분 [   ]
↓
수정부분 [   ]
④
틀린부분 [   ]
↓
수정부분 [   ]
⑤
틀린부분 [   ]
↓
수정부분 [   ]

2022년_고1_9월_인천광역시 교육청_학력평가_24번

7. 다음 글에서 어법상 틀린 부분 5곳을 찾은 뒤, 수정하시오.361)

Many people make a mistake of only operating along the safe zones, and in the process they miss the opportunity to achieve greater things. They are so because a fear of the unknown and a fear of treading the unknown paths of life. Those that are enough brave to take those roads less travelling are able to get great returns and derive major satisfaction out of their courageous moves. Being overcautious will mean that you will miss attaining the greatest levels of your potential. You must learn to take those chances what many people around you will not take, because your success will flow from those bold decisions that you will take along the way.

①
틀린부분　[　　　　　　　　　　]
↓
수정부분　[　　　　　　　　　　]
②
틀린부분　[　　　　　　　　　　]
↓
수정부분　[　　　　　　　　　　]
③
틀린부분　[　　　　　　　　　　]
↓
수정부분　[　　　　　　　　　　]
④
틀린부분　[　　　　　　　　　　]
↓
수정부분　[　　　　　　　　　　]
⑤
틀린부분　[　　　　　　　　　　]
↓
수정부분　[　　　　　　　　　　]

2022년_고1_9월_인천광역시 교육청_학력평가_25번

8. 다음 글에서 어법상 틀린 부분 5곳을 찾은 뒤, 수정하시오.362)

The graph above showing the share of the urban population by continent in 1950 and in 2020. For each continent, the share of the urban population in 2020 was larger than it in 1950. From 1950 to 2020, the share of the urban population in Africa increasing from 14.3% to 43.5%. The share of the urban population in Asia was the second lowest in 1950 but not in 2020. In 1950, the share of the urban population in Europe was larger than those in Latin America and the Caribbean, whereas the reverse was true in 2020. Among the five continents, Northern America was ranking in the first position for the share of the urban population in both 1950 and 2020.

①
틀린부분　[　　　　　　　　　　]
↓
수정부분　[　　　　　　　　　　]
②
틀린부분　[　　　　　　　　　　]
↓
수정부분　[　　　　　　　　　　]
③
틀린부분　[　　　　　　　　　　]
↓
수정부분　[　　　　　　　　　　]
④
틀린부분　[　　　　　　　　　　]
↓
수정부분　[　　　　　　　　　　]
⑤
틀린부분　[　　　　　　　　　　]
↓
수정부분　[　　　　　　　　　　]

2022년_고1_9월_인천광역시 교육청_학력평가_26번

9. 다음 글에서 어법상 틀린 부분 5곳을 찾은 뒤, 수정하시오.363)

Wilbur Smith was a South African novelist specialising in historical fiction. Smith wanted to become a journalist, written about social conditions in South Africa, but his father was never supportive of his writing and forced him getting a real job. Smith studied further and became a tax accountant, but he finally turned back to his love of writing. He wrote his first novel, The Gods First Make Mad, and was received 20 rejections by 1962. In 1964, Smith published another novel, When the Lion Feeds, and it went on to being successful, selling around the world. A famous actor and film producer bought the film rights for When the Lion Feeds, although no movie resulted. By the time of his death in 2021 he had been published 49 novels, selling more than 140 million copies worldwide.

①
틀린부분 [   ]
↓
수정부분 [   ]
②
틀린부분 [   ]
↓
수정부분 [   ]
③
틀린부분 [   ]
↓
수정부분 [   ]
④
틀린부분 [   ]
↓
수정부분 [   ]
⑤
틀린부분 [   ]
↓
수정부분 [   ]

2022년_고1_9월_인천광역시 교육청_학력평가_27번

10. 다음 글에서 어법상 틀린 부분 5곳을 찾은 뒤, 수정하시오.364)

2022 Springfield Park Yoga Class
The popular yoga class in Springfield Park returns! Enjoy yoga hosting the park lawn. Unless you can't make it to the park, join us online on our social media platforms!
◆When: Saturdays, 2 p.m. to 3 p.m., September
◆Registration: At least TWO hours before each class will start, sign up here.
◆Notes
•For online classes: find a quiet space with enough room of you to stretch out.
•For classes in the park: mats are not providing, so bring your own!
※The class will be canceled if the weather is unfavorable. For more information, click here.

①
틀린부분 [   ]
↓
수정부분 [   ]
②
틀린부분 [   ]
↓
수정부분 [   ]
③
틀린부분 [   ]
↓
수정부분 [   ]
④
틀린부분 [   ]
↓
수정부분 [   ]
⑤
틀린부분 [   ]
↓
수정부분 [   ]

2022년_고1_9월_인천광역시 교육청_학력평가_28번

11. 다음 글에서 어법상 틀린 부분 5곳을 찾은 뒤, 수정 하시오.365)

Kenner High School's Water Challenge
Kenner High School's Water Challenge is a new contest proposed measures against water pollution. Please share your ideas for dealing with water pollution!
Submission
How: Submit your proposal by email to admin@khswater.edu.
When: September 5, 2022 to September 23, 2022
Details
Participants must enter in teams of four and can only join with one team.
Submission is limiting to one proposal per teams.
Participants must use the proposal form provide on the website.
Prizes
1st: $50 gift certificate
2nd: $30 gift certificate
3rd: $10 gift certificate
Please visit www.khswater.edu to learn more about the challenge.

①	
틀린부분 [	]
↓	
수정부분 [	]
②	
틀린부분 [	]
↓	
수정부분 [	]
③	
틀린부분 [	]
↓	
수정부분 [	]
④	
틀린부분 [	]
↓	
수정부분 [	]
⑤	
틀린부분 [	]
↓	
수정부분 [	]

2022년_고1_9월_인천광역시 교육청_학력평가_29번

12. 다음 글에서 어법상 틀린 부분 5곳을 찾은 뒤, 수정 하시오.366)

The human brain, it turns out, has been shrunk in mass by about 10 percent since it peaked in size 15,000-30,000 years ago. One possible reason is that many thousands of years ago humans lived in a world of dangerous predators what they had to have their wits about them at all times to avoid to be killed. Today, we have effectively domesticated ourselves and many of the tasks of survival — from avoiding immediate death to building shelters to obtaining food — has been outsourced to the wider society. We are smaller than our ancestors too, and it is a characteristic of domestic animals which they are generally smaller than their wild cousins. None of this may mean we are dumber — brain size is not necessarily an indicator of human intelligence — but it may mean that our brains today are wired up differently, and perhaps more efficiently, than those of our ancestors.

①	
틀린부분 [	]
↓	
수정부분 [	]
②	
틀린부분 [	]
↓	
수정부분 [	]
③	
틀린부분 [	]
↓	
수정부분 [	]
④	
틀린부분 [	]
↓	
수정부분 [	]
⑤	
틀린부분 [	]
↓	
수정부분 [	]

스승의날 영어연구소

2022년_고1_9월_인천광역시 교육청_학력평가_30번

13. 다음 글에서 어법상 틀린 부분 5곳을 찾은 뒤, 수정 하시오.367)

It is widely believed that certain herbs somehow magically improve the work of certain organs, and "cure" specific diseases as a result. Such statements are unscientific and groundless. Sometimes herbs are appeared to work, since they tend to increase your blood circulation in an aggressive attempt by your body to eliminate them from your system. That can create a temporary feeling of a high, that makes it seem as if your health condition has improved. Also, herbs can have a placebo effect, just like any other method, thus helped you feel better. Whatever the case, it is your body which has the intelligence to regain health, and not the herbs. How can herbs have the intelligence needed to direct your body into getting healthier? That is impossible. Try to imagine how herbs might be come into your body and intelligently fix your problems. If you try to do that, you will see how impossible it seems. Otherwise, it would mean that herbs are more intelligent than the human body, which is truly hard to believe.

*placebo effect: 위약 효과

①
틀린부분 [   ]
↓
수정부분 [   ]

②
틀린부분 [   ]
↓
수정부분 [   ]

③
틀린부분 [   ]
↓
수정부분 [   ]

④
틀린부분 [   ]
↓
수정부분 [   ]

⑤
틀린부분 [   ]
↓
수정부분 [   ]

2022년_고1_9월_인천광역시 교육청_학력평가_31번

14. 다음 글에서 어법상 틀린 부분 5곳을 찾은 뒤, 수정 하시오.368)

We worry that the robots are taking our jobs, but just as common a problem is that the robots are taking our judgment. In the large warehouses so common behind the scenes of today's economy, human 'pickers' hurry around grabbing products off shelves and moving them to where they can be packed and dispatch. In their ears are headpieces: the voice of 'Jennifer', a piece of software, tell them where to go and what to do, controls the smallest details of their movements. Jennifer breaks down instructions into tiny chunks, to minimise error and maximise productivity — for example, rather than picking eighteen copies of a book off a shelf, the human worker would be politely instructed to pick five. Then another five. Then yet another five. Then another three. Working in such conditions reduce people to machines made of flesh. Rather than asking us to think or adapt, the Jennifer unit takes over the thought process and treating workers as an inexpensive source of some visual processing and a pair of opposable thumbs.

*dispatch: 발송하다 **chunk: 덩어리

①
틀린부분 [   ]
↓
수정부분 [   ]

②
틀린부분 [   ]
↓
수정부분 [   ]

③
틀린부분 [   ]
↓
수정부분 [   ]

④
틀린부분 [   ]
↓
수정부분 [   ]

⑤
틀린부분 [   ]
↓
수정부분 [   ]

2022년_고1_9월_인천광역시 교육청_학력평가_32번

15. 다음 글에서 어법상 틀린 부분 5곳을 찾은 뒤, 수정 하시오.369)

The prevailed view among developmental scientists are that people are active contributors to their own development. People are influenced by the physical and social contexts which they live, but they also play a role in influencing their development by interacting with, and changing, those contexts. Even infants influence the world around them and construct their own development through their interactions. Consider an infant who smiles at each adult he sees; he influences his world because adults are likely to smiling, use "baby talk," and play with him in response. The infant brings adults into close contact, making one-on-one interactions and creating opportunities for learning. By engaging the world around them, thinking, being curious, and interact with people, objects, and the world around them, individuals of all ages are "manufacturers of their own development."

①

틀린부분 [   ]

↓

수정부분 [   ]

②

틀린부분 [   ]

↓

수정부분 [   ]

③

틀린부분 [   ]

↓

수정부분 [   ]

④

틀린부분 [   ]

↓

수정부분 [   ]

⑤

틀린부분 [   ]

↓

수정부분 [   ]

2022년_고1_9월_인천광역시 교육청_학력평가_33번

16. 다음 글에서 어법상 틀린 부분 5곳을 찾은 뒤, 수정 하시오.370)

The demand for freshness can have hiding environmental costs. While freshness is now being used as a term in food marketing as part of a return to nature, the demand for year-round supplies of fresh produce such as soft fruit and exotic vegetables have led to the widespread use of hot houses in cold climates and increasing reliance on total quality control — management by temperature control, use of pesticides and computer/satellite-based logistics. The demand for freshness has also contributed to concerns about food wastage. Use of 'best before', 'sell by' and 'eat by' labels has legally allowed institutional waste. Campaigners have been exposed the scandal of overproduction and waste. Tristram Stuart, one of the global band of anti-waste campaigner, argues that, with freshly made sandwiches, over-ordering is standard practice across the retail sector to avoid the appearance of empty shelf space, led to high volumes of waste when supply regularly exceeds demand.

* pesticide: 살충제 ** logistics: 물류, 유통

①

틀린부분 [   ]

↓

수정부분 [   ]

②

틀린부분 [   ]

↓

수정부분 [   ]

③

틀린부분 [   ]

↓

수정부분 [   ]

④

틀린부분 [   ]

↓

수정부분 [   ]

⑤

틀린부분 [   ]

↓

수정부분 [   ]

17. 다음 글에서 어법상 틀린 부분 5곳을 찾은 뒤, 수정하시오.371)

In the studies of Colin Cherry at the Massachusetts Institute for Technology back in the 1950s, his participants listened to voices in one ear at a time and then through both ears in an effort to determine what we can listen to two people talked at the same time. One ear always contained a message that the listener had to repeat back (called "shadowing") while the other ear included people speaking. The trick was to seeing if you could totally focus on the main message and also hear someone talking in your other ear. Cleverly, Cherry found it was impossible of his participants to know whether the message in the other ear was speaking by a man or woman, in English or another language, or was even comprised of real words at all! In other words, people could not process two pieces of information at the same time.

①
틀린부분 [   ]
↓
수정부분 [   ]

②
틀린부분 [   ]
↓
수정부분 [   ]

③
틀린부분 [   ]
↓
수정부분 [   ]

④
틀린부분 [   ]
↓
수정부분 [   ]

⑤
틀린부분 [   ]
↓
수정부분 [   ]

18. 다음 글에서 어법상 틀린 부분 5곳을 찾은 뒤, 수정하시오.372)

The fast-paced evolution of Information and Communication Technologies (ICTs) has radically been transformed the dynamics and business models of the tourism and hospitality industry. This leads to new levels/forms of competitiveness among service providers and transforms the customer experience through new services. Creating unique experiences and providing convenient services to customers lead to satisfaction and, eventually, customer loyalty to the service provider or brand (i.e., hotels). In particular, the most recent technological boost receiving by the tourism sector are represented by mobile applications. Indeed, empowering tourists with mobile access to services such as hotel reservations, airline ticketing, and recommendations for local attractions generated strong interest and considerable profits.

* hospitality industry: 서비스업(호텔·식당업 등)

①
틀린부분 [   ]
↓
수정부분 [   ]

②
틀린부분 [   ]
↓
수정부분 [   ]

③
틀린부분 [   ]
↓
수정부분 [   ]

④
틀린부분 [   ]
↓
수정부분 [   ]

⑤
틀린부분 [   ]
↓
수정부분 [   ]

2022년_고1_9월_인천광역시 교육청_학력평가_36번

19. 다음 글에서 어법상 틀린 부분 5곳을 찾은 뒤, 수정하시오. 373)

With nearly a billion hungry people in the world, there is obviously no single cause. However, far and away the biggest cause is poverty. Seventy-nine percent of the world's hungry lives in nations what are net exporters of food. How can this be? The reason people are hungry in those countries is that the products produced there can be sold on the world market for more than the local citizens can afford to paying for them. In the modern age you do not starve because you have no food, you starve because you have no money. So the problem really is which food is, in the grand scheme of things, too expensive and many people are too poor buying it. The answer will be in continuing the trend of lowering the cost of food.

* net exporter: 순 수출국 ** scheme: 체계, 조직

①
틀린부분 [   ]
↓
수정부분 [   ]
②
틀린부분 [   ]
↓
수정부분 [   ]
③
틀린부분 [   ]
↓
수정부분 [   ]
④
틀린부분 [   ]
↓
수정부분 [   ]
⑤
틀린부분 [   ]
↓
수정부분 [   ]

2022년_고1_9월_인천광역시 교육청_학력평가_37번

20. 다음 글에서 어법상 틀린 부분 5곳을 찾은 뒤, 수정하시오. 374)

Most people have a perfect time of day when they feel they are at their best, whether in the morning, evening, or afternoon. Some of us are night owls, some early birds, and others in between may feel most actively during the afternoon hours. If you are able to organize your day and divide your work, make it a point to deal with tasks what demand attention at your best time of the day. However, if the task you face demand creativity and novel ideas, it's best to tackle it at your "worst" time of day! So if you are an early bird, make sure to attack your creative task in the evening, and vice versa for night owls. When your mind and body are less alert than at your "peak" hours, the muse of creativity awakens and is allowed to roam more free. In other words, when your mental machinery is loose rather than standing at attention, the creativity is flowed.

*roam: (어슬렁어슬렁) 거닐다

①
틀린부분 [   ]
↓
수정부분 [   ]
②
틀린부분 [   ]
↓
수정부분 [   ]
③
틀린부분 [   ]
↓
수정부분 [   ]
④
틀린부분 [   ]
↓
수정부분 [   ]
⑤
틀린부분 [   ]
↓
수정부분 [   ]

2022년_고1_9월_인천광역시 교육청_학력평가_38번

21. 다음 글에서 어법상 틀린 부분 5곳을 찾은 뒤, 수정 하시오.375)

Television is the number one leisure activity in the United States and Europe, consumed more than half of our free time. We generally think of television as a way to relax, tune out, and escape from our troubles for a bit each day. During this is true, there is increasing evidence that we are more motivated to tune in to our favorite shows and characters when we are feeling lonely or have a greater need for social connection. Television watching does satisfies these social needs to some extent, at least in the short run. Unfortunately, it is also likely to "crowd out" other activities in which produce more sustainable social contributions to our social well-being. The most television we watch, the less likely we are to volunteer our time or to spend time with people in our social networks. In other words, the more time we make for Friends, the less time we have for friends in real life.

*Friends: 프렌즈(미국의 한 방송국에서 방영된 시트콤)

①
틀린부분 [   ]
↓
수정부분 [   ]
②
틀린부분 [   ]
↓
수정부분 [   ]
③
틀린부분 [   ]
↓
수정부분 [   ]
④
틀린부분 [   ]
↓
수정부분 [   ]
⑤
틀린부분 [   ]
↓
수정부분 [   ]

2022년_고1_9월_인천광역시 교육청_학력평가_39번

22. 다음 글에서 어법상 틀린 부분 5곳을 찾은 뒤, 수정 하시오.376)

We often associate the concept of temperature with how hot or cold feels an object when we touch it. In this way, our senses provide us with a qualitative indication of temperature. Our senses, however, are unreliable and often mislead us. For example, if you stand in bare feet with one foot on carpet and the other on a tile floor, the tile feels colder than the carpet despite both are at the same temperature. The two objects feel differently because tile transfers energy by heat at a higher rate than carpet is. Your skin "measures" the rate of energy transfer by heat rather than the actual temperature. What we need is a reliable and reproducible method for measuring the relative hotness or coldness of objects rather than the rate of energy transfer. Scientists have been developed a variety of thermometers for making such quantitative measurements.

*thermometer: 온도계

①
틀린부분 [   ]
↓
수정부분 [   ]
②
틀린부분 [   ]
↓
수정부분 [   ]
③
틀린부분 [   ]
↓
수정부분 [   ]
④
틀린부분 [   ]
↓
수정부분 [   ]
⑤
틀린부분 [   ]
↓
수정부분 [   ]

2022년_고1_9월_인천광역시 교육청_학력평가_40번

23. 다음 글에서 어법상 틀린 부분 5곳을 찾은 뒤, 수정하시오.377)

My colleagues and I ran an experiment testing two different messages meant to convince thousands of resistant alumni making a donation. One message emphasized the opportunity to do good: donating would benefit students, faculty, and staff. The other emphasized the opportunity to feel good: donors would enjoy the warm glow of giving. The two messages were equally effective: in both cases, 6.5 percent of the unwilling alumni ended up donated. Then we combined them, because of two reasons are better than one. Except they didn't. When we put the two reasons together, the giving rate dropped below 3 percent. Each reason alone was more than twice as effective as the two combined. The audience was already skeptical. When we gave them different kinds of reasons to donate, we triggered their awareness which someone was trying to persuade them — and they shielded themselves against it.

* alumni: 졸업생 ** skeptical: 회의적인

↓

In the experiment mentioned above, when the two different reasons to donate were given simultaneously, the audience was less likely to be convinced because they could recognize the intention to persuade them.

①
틀린부분 [　　　　　　　　　　]
↓
수정부분 [　　　　　　　　　　]
②
틀린부분 [　　　　　　　　　　]
↓
수정부분 [　　　　　　　　　　]
③
틀린부분 [　　　　　　　　　　]
↓
수정부분 [　　　　　　　　　　]
④
틀린부분 [　　　　　　　　　　]
↓
수정부분 [　　　　　　　　　　]
⑤
틀린부분 [　　　　　　　　　　]
↓
수정부분 [　　　　　　　　　　]

2022년_고1_9월_인천광역시 교육청_학력평가_41~42번

24. 다음 글에서 어법상 틀린 부분 5곳을 찾은 뒤, 수정하시오.378)

In a society that rejects the consumption of insects there are some individuals who overcome this rejection, but most will continue with this attitude. That may be very difficult to convince an entire society what insects are totally suitable for consumption. However, there are examples in which this reversal of attitudes about certain foods have happened to an entire society. Several examples in the past 120 years from European-American society are: considering lobster a luxury food instead of a food for servants and prisoners; considering sushi a safe and delicious food; and considering pizza not just a food for the rural poor of Sicily. In Latin American countries, which insects are already consumed, a portion of the population hates their consumption and associates it with poverty. There are also examples of people who have had the habit of consuming them and abandoned that habit due to shame, and because they do not want to categorize as poor or uncivilized. According to Esther Katz, an anthropologist, if the consumption of insects as a food luxury is to be promoted, there would be more chances that some individuals who do not present this habit overcome ideas under which they were educated. And this could also help to revalue the consumption of insects by those people who already eat them

①
틀린부분 [　　　　　　　　　　]
↓
수정부분 [　　　　　　　　　　]
②
틀린부분 [　　　　　　　　　　]
↓
수정부분 [　　　　　　　　　　]
③
틀린부분 [　　　　　　　　　　]
↓
수정부분 [　　　　　　　　　　]
④
틀린부분 [　　　　　　　　　　]
↓
수정부분 [　　　　　　　　　　]
⑤
틀린부분 [　　　　　　　　　　]
↓
수정부분 [　　　　　　　　　　]

서술형 Lv_기본

2022년_고1_9월_인천광역시 교육청_학력평가_18번

Dear Parents/Guardians, Class parties will be held on the afternoon December 16th, 2022. Children may bring in sweets, crisps, biscuits, cakes, and drinks. We are requesting that children do not bring in home-cooked or prepared food. (A) 모든 음식은 성분을 명확하게 목록으로 작성하여 밀봉된 꾸러미로 가져와야 합니다. Fruit and vegetables are welcomed if they are pre-packed in a sealed packet from the shop. Please DO NOT send any food into school containing nuts as we have many children with severe nut allergies. Please check (B) [bring / children / careful / food / your / the ingredients / all / of]. Thank you for your continued support and cooperation.

Yours sincerely, Lisa Brown, Headteacher

1. 위 글의 밑줄 친 (A)의 우리말과 같도록 아래의 〈조건〉을 활용한 뒤 〈보기〉의 단어를 알맞게 영작하시오.379)

〈조건〉
1. 과거분사를 사용할 것
2. 〈보기〉의 단어를 모두 사용하되, 필요시 변형 또는 추가하여 13단어로 쓸 것
(단, 동사는 기본형태이므로, 반드시 어형변화 해야 함)
〈보기〉
list / seal / ingredients / packet

〈답〉

2. 위 글의 제목을 주어진 〈보기〉를 활용하여 서술하시오.380)

〈보기〉
Attending / Class / Parties / Precautions / for

〈답〉

3. 위 글의 밑줄 친 (B)에 주어진 단어를 활용하여 알맞게 영작하시오.381)

〈답〉

2022년_고1_9월_인천광역시 교육청_학력평가_19번

It was two hours before the submission deadline and I still hadn't finished my news article. I sat at the desk, but suddenly, the typewriter didn't work. (A) 내가 아무리 세게 키를 두드려도, 레버는 종이를 두드리려 움직이지 않았다. I started to realize that I would not be able to finish the article on time. Desperately, I rested the typewriter on my lap and started hitting each key with as much force as I could manage. Nothing happened. (B) [of / have / happened / something / might / inside / thinking / it]. I opened the cover, lifted up the keys, and found the problem — a paper clip. The keys had no room to move. After picking it out, I pressed and pulled some parts. The keys moved smoothly again. I breathed deeply and smiled. Now I knew that I could finish my article on time.

4. 위 글의 밑줄 친 (A)의 우리말과 같도록 아래의 〈조건〉을 활용한 뒤 〈보기〉의 단어를 알맞게 영작하시오.382)

〈조건〉
1. no matter ~ 구문을 사용할 것
2. 〈보기〉의 단어를 모두 사용하되, 필요시 변형 또는 추가하여 16단어로 쓸 것
(단, 동사는 기본형태이므로, 반드시 어형변화 해야 함)
〈보기〉
hard / strike / levers / matter / tap / how

〈답〉

5. 위 글의 제목을 주어진 〈보기〉를 활용하여 서술하시오.383)

〈보기〉
Is / Not / Working? / The / Typewriter / Why

〈답〉

6. 위 글의 밑줄 친 (B)에 주어진 단어를 활용하여 알맞게 영작하시오.384)

〈답〉

2022년_고1_9월_인천광역시 교육청_학력평가_20번

Experts on writing say, "Get rid of as many words as possible." Each word must do something important. If it doesn't, get rid of it. Well, this doesn't work for speaking. (A) <u>말을 할 때는 아이디어를 소개하고, 표현하며, 적절히 부연 설명하는 데 글을 쓸 때보다 더 많은 단어가 필요하다.</u> Why is this so? While the reader can reread, the listener cannot rehear. Speakers do not come equipped with a replay button. Because listeners are easily distracted, they will miss many pieces of what a speaker says. If they miss the crucial sentence, they may never catch up. (B) [necessary / their / longer / this / about / for / to / it / points / makes / talk / speakers] using more words on them than would be used to express the same idea in writing.

7. 위 글의 밑줄 친 (A)의 우리말과 같도록 아래의 〈조건〉을 활용한 뒤 〈보기〉의 단어를 알맞게 영작하시오.385)

〈조건〉

1. 가주어(it)-진주어(that절) 구문을 사용할 것
2. 〈보기〉의 단어를 모두 사용하되, 필요시 변형 또는 추가하여 19단어로 쓸 것
(단, 동사는 기본형태이므로, 반드시 어형변화 해야 함)

〈보기〉

take / elaborate / speech / take/ adequately / express

〈답〉

8. 위 글의 제목을 주어진 〈보기〉를 활용하여 서술하시오.386)

〈보기〉

Better / Words / Speech / a / Make / More

〈답〉

9. 위 글의 밑줄 친 (B)에 주어진 단어를 활용하여 알맞게 영작하시오.387)

〈답〉

2022년_고1_9월_인천광역시 교육청_학력평가_21번

Is the customer always right? When customers return a broken product to a famous company, which makes kitchen and bathroom fixtures, the company nearly always offers a replacement to maintain good customer relations. (A) <u>그럼에도, 그 회사의 상품 보증 전문가는 상품이 멀쩡하거나 남용되었을 때와 같이, "'안 돼요.'라고 말을 해야 할 때가 있다."고 설명한다.</u> Entrepreneur Lauren Thorp, who owns an e-commerce company, says, "While the customer is 'always' right, sometimes you just have to fire a customer." When Thorp has tried everything to resolve a complaint and realizes that the customer will be dissatisfied no matter what, she returns her (B) [who / to / attention / are / the rest / customers, / her / "the reason for my success," / of / says / she].

10. 위 글의 밑줄 친 (A)의 우리말과 같도록 아래의 〈조건〉을 활용한 뒤 〈보기〉의 단어를 알맞게 영작하시오.388)

〈조건〉

1. 현재완료 수동태를 사용할 것
2. 〈보기〉의 단어를 모두 사용하되, 필요시 변형 또는 추가하여 27단어로 쓸 것
(단, 동사는 기본형태이므로, 반드시 어형변화 해야 함)

〈보기〉

explain / undamage / abuse / warranty / product

〈답〉

11. 위 글의 제목을 주어진 〈보기〉를 활용하여 서술하시오.389)

〈보기〉

Always / The / Right? / Is / Customer

〈답〉

12. 위 글의 밑줄 친 (B)에 주어진 단어를 활용하여 알맞게 영작하시오.390)

〈답〉

2022년_고1_9월_인천광역시 교육청_학력평가_22번

A recent study from Carnegie Mellon University in Pittsburgh, called "When Too Much of a Good Thing May Be Bad," indicates that classrooms with too much decoration are a source of distraction for young children and directly affect their cognitive performance. (A) 시각적으로 지나치게 자극되었을 때, 아이들은 집중하는 데 많이 어려워하고 결국 더 나쁜 학습 결과로 끝이 난다. On the other hand, if there is not much decoration on the classroom walls, the children are less distracted, spend more time on their activities, and learn more. So it's our job, in order to support their attention, (B) [it / and / the right / balance / decoration / to / the complete / excessive / find / absence / between / of].

13. 위 글의 밑줄 친 (A)의 우리말과 같도록 아래의 <조건>을 활용한 뒤 <보기>의 단어를 알맞게 영작하시오.391)

<조건>
1. 비교급을 사용할 것
2. <보기>의 단어를 모두 사용하되, 필요시 변형 또는 추가하여 19단어로 쓸 것
(단, 동사는 기본형태이므로, 반드시 어형변화 해야 함)

<보기>
be / concentrate / have / deal / overstimulate / academic

<답>

14. 위 글의 제목을 주어진 <보기>를 활용하여 서술하시오.392)

<보기>
Medicine? / Poison / Decoration: / Classroom / or

<답>

15. 위 글의 밑줄 친 (B)에 주어진 단어를 활용하여 알맞게 영작하시오.393)

<답>

2022년_고1_9월_인천광역시 교육청_학력평가_23번

For creatures like us, evolution smiled upon those with a strong need to belong. Survival and reproduction are the criteria of success by natural selection, and forming relationships with other people can be useful for both survival and reproduction. Groups can share resources, care for sick members, scare off predators, fight together against enemies, divide tasks so as to improve efficiency, and contribute to survival in many other ways. (A) 특히, 한 개인과 한 집단이 같은 자원을 원하면, 집단이 일반적으로 이기고, 그래서 자원에 대한 경쟁은 소속하려는 욕구를 특별히 좋아할 것이다. Belongingness will likewise promote reproduction, such as by bringing potential mates into contact with each other, and in particular by keeping parents together to care for their children, (B) [more / are / one / who / more / than / to / much / survive / if / likely / they / caregiver / have].

16. 위 글의 밑줄 친 (A)의 우리말과 같도록 아래의 <조건>을 활용한 뒤 <보기>의 단어를 알맞게 영작하시오.394)

<조건>
1. to부정사를 사용할 것
2. <보기>의 단어를 모두 사용하되, 필요시 변형 또는 추가하여 28단어로 쓸 것
(단, 동사는 기본형태이므로, 반드시 어형변화 해야 함)

<보기>
resource / belong / competition / individual / prevail / favor / need / generally

<답>

17. 위 글의 제목을 주어진 <보기>를 활용하여 서술하시오.395)

<보기>
Belonging / of / The / Help / Evolutionary

<답>

18. 위 글의 밑줄 친 (B)에 주어진 단어를 활용하여 알맞게 영작하시오.396)

<답>

2022년_고1_9월_인천광역시 교육청_학력평가_24번

Many people make a mistake of only operating along the safe zones, and in the process they miss the opportunity to achieve greater things. They do so because of a fear of the unknown and a fear of treading the unknown paths of life. Those that are brave enough to take those roads less travelled are able to get great returns and derive major satisfaction out of their courageous moves. Being overcautious will mean that you will miss attaining the greatest levels of your potential. (A) <u>여러분은 주변에 있는 많은 사람들이 선택하지 않을 기회를 택하는 것을 배워야 한다</u>, because your success will flow from (B) [along / way / from / decisions / those / bold / take / you / the / that / will].

19. 위 글의 밑줄 친 (A)의 우리말과 같도록 아래의 〈조건〉을 활용한 뒤 〈보기〉의 단어를 알맞게 영작하시오.397)

〈조건〉

1. 관계대명사를 사용할 것
2. 〈보기〉의 단어를 모두 사용하되, 필요시 변형 또는 추가하여 15단어로 쓸 것
(단, 동사는 기본형태이므로, 반드시 어형변화 해야 함)

〈보기〉

learn / take / chances / those / must

〈답〉

20. 위 글의 제목을 주어진 〈보기〉를 활용하여 서술하시오.398)

〈보기〉

for / Take / Success / to / Need / You / What

〈답〉

21. 위 글의 밑줄 친 (B)에 주어진 단어를 활용하여 알맞게 영작하시오.399)

〈답〉

2022년_고1_9월_인천광역시 교육청_학력평가_29번

The human brain, it turns out, has shrunk in mass by about 10 percent since it peaked in size 15,000-30,000 years ago. One possible reason is that many thousands of years ago humans lived in a world of dangerous predators where they had to have their wits about them at all times to avoid being killed. Today, we have effectively domesticated ourselves and many of the tasks of survival — from avoiding immediate death to building shelters to obtaining food — have been outsourced to the wider society. (A) <u>우리는 우리의 조상보다 더 작기도 한데, 가축이 그들의 야생 사촌보다 일반적으로 더 작다는 것은 가축의 한 특징이다.</u> None of this may mean we are dumber — brain size is not necessarily an indicator of human intelligence — (B) [differently / that / it / wired / are / up / brains / today / may / but / our / mean], and perhaps more efficiently, than those of our ancestors.

22. 위 글의 밑줄 친 (A)의 우리말과 같도록 아래의 〈조건〉을 활용한 뒤 〈보기〉의 단어를 알맞게 영작하시오.400)

〈조건〉

1. 가주어(it)-진주어(that절) 구문을 사용할 것
2. 〈보기〉의 단어를 모두 사용하되, 필요시 변형 또는 추가하여 24단어로 쓸 것
(단, 동사는 기본형태이므로, 반드시 어형변화 해야 함)

〈보기〉

small / domestic / cousins / wild / ancestors

〈답〉

23. 위 글의 제목을 주어진 〈보기〉를 활용하여 서술하시오.401)

〈보기〉

The / Changes / Brain / Due / to / Size / in / Environment

〈답〉

24. 위 글의 밑줄 친 (B)에 주어진 단어를 활용하여 알맞게 영작하시오.402)

〈답〉

2022년_고1_9월_인천광역시 교육청_학력평가_30번

It is widely believed that certain herbs somehow magically improve the work of certain organs, and "cure" specific diseases as a result. Such statements are unscientific and groundless. Sometimes herbs appear to work, since they tend to increase your blood circulation in an aggressive attempt by your body to eliminate them from your system. That can create a temporary feeling of a high, which makes it seem as if your health condition has improved. Also, herbs can have a placebo effect, just like any other method, thus helping you feel better. (A) 어떠한 경우든, 건강을 되찾게 하는 지성을 가진 것은 허브가 아니라 바로 당신의 몸이다. How can herbs have the intelligence needed to direct your body into getting healthier? That is impossible. Try to imagine (B) [might / come / and / into / body / fix / intelligently / problems / herbs / your / how / your]. If you try to do that, you will see how impossible it seems. Otherwise, it would mean that herbs are more intelligent than the human body, which is truly hard to believe.

*placebo effect: 위약 효과

25. 위 글의 밑줄 친 (A)의 우리말과 같도록 아래의 〈조건〉을 활용한 뒤 〈보기〉의 단어를 알맞게 영작하시오.403)

〈조건〉
1. 가주어(it)-진주어(that절) 구문을 사용할 것
2. 〈보기〉의 단어를 모두 사용하되, 필요시 변형 또는 추가하여 15단어로 쓸 것
(단, 동사는 기본형태이므로, 반드시 어형변화 해야 함)

〈보기〉
regain / health / intelligence / herbs / whatever

〈답〉

26. 위 글의 제목을 주어진 〈보기〉를 활용하여 서술하시오.404)

〈보기〉
It / Is / Herb: / Panacea / Not / a

〈답〉

27. 위 글의 밑줄 친 (B)에 주어진 단어를 활용하여 알맞게 영작하시오.405)

〈답〉

2022년_고1_9월_인천광역시 교육청_학력평가_31번

We worry that the robots are taking our jobs, but just as common a problem is that the robots are taking our judgment. In the large warehouses so common behind the scenes of today's economy, human 'pickers' hurry around grabbing products off shelves and moving them to where they can be packed and dispatched. (A) 그들의 귀에는 헤드폰이 있는데, 한 소프트웨어 프로그램인 'Jennifer'의 목소리가 그들의 움직임의 가장 작은 세부 사항들을 조종하면서, 그들에게 어디로 갈지와 무엇을 할지를 말한다. Jennifer breaks down instructions into tiny chunks, to minimise error and maximise productivity — for example, rather than picking eighteen copies of a book off a shelf, the human worker would be politely instructed to pick five. Then another five. Then yet another five. Then another three. Working in such conditions reduces people to machines made of flesh. (B) [think / asking / rather / or / than / to / us / adapt], the Jennifer unit takes over the thought process and treats workers as an inexpensive source of some visual processing and a pair of opposable thumbs.

*dispatch: 발송하다 **chunk: 덩어리

28. 위 글의 밑줄 친 (A)의 우리말과 같도록 아래의 〈조건〉을 활용한 뒤 〈보기〉의 단어를 알맞게 영작하시오.406)

〈조건〉
1. 의문사 to 부정사 구문을 사용할 것
2. 〈보기〉의 단어를 모두 사용하되, 필요시 변형 또는 추가하여 29단어로 쓸 것
(단, 동사는 기본형태이므로, 반드시 어형변화 해야 함)

〈보기〉
headpieces / software / control / movements / where / smallest / tell / what / them

〈답〉

29. 위 글의 제목을 주어진 〈보기〉를 활용하여 서술하시오.407)

〈보기〉
from / Robots / What / Take / Humans

〈답〉

30. 위 글의 밑줄 친 (B)에 주어진 단어를 활용하여 알맞게 영작하시오.408)

〈답〉

2022년_고1_9월_인천광역시 교육청_학력평가_32번

The prevailing view among developmental scientists is that people are active contributors to their own development. People are influenced by the physical and social contexts in which they live, but they also play a role in influencing their development by interacting with, and changing, those contexts. Even infants influence the world around them and construct their own development through their interactions. Consider an infant who smiles at each adult he sees; he influences his world because adults are likely to smile, use "baby talk," and play with him in response. (A) <u>그 유아는 어른들을 친밀한 연결로 끌어들여서, 일대일 상호작용을 하고 학습의 기회를 만든다.</u> (B) <u>[curious, and / around / people, / thinking, / them / engaging / interacting / the world / objects, / and / around / by / with / them, / being / the world].</u> individuals of all ages are "manufacturers of their own development."

31. 위 글의 밑줄 친 (A)의 우리말과 같도록 아래의 〈조건〉을 활용한 뒤 〈보기〉의 단어를 알맞게 영작하시오.409)

〈조건〉
1. 분사구문을 사용할 것 2. 〈보기〉의 단어를 모두 사용하되, 필요시 변형 또는 추가하여 15단어로 쓸 것 (단, 동사는 기본형태이므로, 반드시 어형변화 해야 함)
〈보기〉
infant / opportunities / learn / make / create / bring
〈답〉

32. 위 글의 제목을 주어진 〈보기〉를 활용하여 서술하시오.410)

〈보기〉
Our / Contributes / What / Development? / to
〈답〉

33. 위 글의 밑줄 친 (B)에 주어진 단어를 활용하여 알맞게 영작하시오.411)

〈답〉

2022년_고1_9월_인천광역시 교육청_학력평가_33번

The demand for freshness can have hidden environmental costs. (A) <u>자연으로의 회귀의 일부로써 현재 신선함이 식품 마케팅에서 하나의 용어로 사용되고 있는 반면에,</u> the demand for year-round supplies of fresh produce such as soft fruit and exotic vegetables has led to the widespread use of hot houses in cold climates and increasing reliance on total quality control — management by temperature control, use of pesticides and computer/satellite-based logistics. The demand for freshness has also contributed to concerns about food wastage. Use of 'best before', 'sell by' and 'eat by' labels has legally allowed institutional waste. Campaigners have exposed the scandal of overproduction and waste. Tristram Stuart, one of the global band of anti-waste campaigners, argues that, (B) <u>[sandwiches / freshly / made / with],</u> over-ordering is standard practice across the retail sector to avoid the appearance of empty shelf space, leading to high volumes of waste when supply regularly exceeds demand.

* pesticide: 살충제 ** logistics: 물류, 유통

34. 위 글의 밑줄 친 (A)의 우리말과 같도록 아래의 〈조건〉을 활용한 뒤 〈보기〉의 단어를 알맞게 영작하시오.412)

〈조건〉
1. 진행형 수동태를 사용할 것 2. 〈보기〉의 단어를 모두 사용하되, 필요시 변형 또는 추가하여 19단어로 쓸 것 (단, 동사는 기본형태이므로, 반드시 어형변화 해야 함)
〈보기〉
be / use / freshness / marketing / return / nature
〈답〉

35. 위 글의 제목을 주어진 〈보기〉를 활용하여 서술하시오.413)

〈보기〉
The / in / Hidden / Price / Freshness
〈답〉

36. 위 글의 밑줄 친 (B)에 주어진 단어를 활용하여 알맞게 영작하시오.414)

〈답〉

2022년_고1_9월_인천광역시 교육청_학력평가_34번

In the studies of Colin Cherry at the Massachusetts Institute for Technology back in the 1950s, his participants listened to voices in one ear at a time and then through both ears in an effort to determine (B) [two / we / to / the / can / listen / whether / talk / at / people / same / time]. (A) 한쪽 귀로는 듣는 사람이 다시 반복해야 하는 메시지를 계속 들려주었고 다른 한쪽 귀로는 사람들이 말하는 것을 들려주었다. The trick was to see if you could totally focus on the main message and also hear someone talking in your other ear. Cleverly, Cherry found it was impossible for his participants to know whether the message in the other ear was spoken by a man or woman, in English or another language, or was even comprised of real words at all! In other words, people could not process two pieces of information at the same time.

37. 위 글의 밑줄 친 (A)의 우리말과 같도록 아래의 〈조건〉을 활용한 뒤 〈보기〉의 단어를 알맞게 영작하시오.415)

〈조건〉
1. 관계대명사를 사용할 것
2. 〈보기〉의 단어를 모두 사용하되, 필요시 변형 또는 추가하여 20단어로 쓸 것
(단, 동사는 기본형태이므로, 반드시 어형변화 해야 함)

〈보기〉
include / speak / repeat / contain / message / have

〈답〉

38. 위 글의 제목을 주어진 〈보기〉를 활용하여 서술하시오.416)

〈보기〉
about / People's / Information / Interesting / What / Is / Processing

〈답〉

39. 위 글의 밑줄 친 (B)에 주어진 단어를 활용하여 알맞게 영작하시오.417)

〈답〉

2022년_고1_9월_인천광역시 교육청_학력평가_35번

The fast-paced evolution of Information and Communication Technologies (ICTs) has radically transformed the dynamics and business models of the tourism and hospitality industry. This leads to new levels/forms of competitiveness among service providers and transforms the customer experience through new services. Creating unique experiences and providing convenient services to customers leads to satisfaction and, eventually, customer loyalty to the service provider or brand (i.e., hotels). (A) 특히, 관광업 분야에서 받아들여진 가장 최근의 상승은 모바일 애플리케이션에 의해 대표된다. Indeed, (B) [with / ticketing, / and / for / interest / services / mobile / to / hotel / generates / considerable / airline / attractions / strong / profits / recommendations / empowering / reservations, / as / local / tourists / access / and / such].

* hospitality industry: 서비스업(호텔·식당업 등)

40. 위 글의 밑줄 친 (A)의 우리말과 같도록 아래의 〈조건〉을 활용한 뒤 〈보기〉의 단어를 알맞게 영작하시오.418)

〈조건〉
1. 과거분사를 사용할 것
2. 〈보기〉의 단어를 모두 사용하되, 필요시 변형 또는 추가하여 17단어로 쓸 것
(단, 동사는 기본형태이므로, 반드시 어형변화 해야 함)

〈보기〉
tourism / applications / boost / receive / represent / recent / sector

〈답〉

41. 위 글의 제목을 주어진 〈보기〉를 활용하여 서술하시오.419)

〈보기〉
Butterfly / Technology / and / Evolution / Effect / of

〈답〉

42. 위 글의 밑줄 친 (B)에 주어진 단어를 활용하여 알맞게 영작하시오.420)

〈답〉

2022년_고1_9월_인천광역시 교육청_학력평가_36번

With nearly a billion hungry people in the world, there is obviously no single cause. However, far and away the biggest cause is poverty. (A) <u>세계의 굶주린 사람들의 79퍼센트가 식량 순 수출국에 살고 있다.</u> How can this be? The reason people are hungry in those countries is that the products produced there can be sold on the world market for more than the local citizens can afford to pay for them. In the modern age you do not starve because you have no food, you starve because you have no money. So the problem really is that food is, in the grand scheme of things, too expensive and (B) <u>[are / it / many / to / poor / buy / too / people].</u> The answer will be in continuing the trend of lowering the cost of food.

* net exporter: 순 수출국 ** scheme: 체계, 조직

---

43. 위 글의 밑줄 친 (A)의 우리말과 같도록 아래의 〈조건〉을 활용한 뒤 〈보기〉의 단어를 알맞게 영작하시오. 421)

〈조건〉
1. 관계대명사를 사용할 것
2. 〈보기〉의 단어를 모두 사용하되, 필요시 변형 또는 추가하여 15단어로 쓸 것
(단, 동사는 기본형태이므로, 반드시 어형변화 해야 함)

〈보기〉
hungry / exporters / live / nations / net

〈답〉

---

44. 위 글의 제목을 주어진 〈보기〉를 활용하여 서술하시오. 422)

〈보기〉
Not / Cause / Food / Are / Poverty: / The / Shortages

〈답〉

---

45. 위 글의 밑줄 친 (B)에 주어진 단어를 활용하여 알맞게 영작하시오. 423)

〈답〉

2022년_고1_9월_인천광역시 교육청_학력평가_37번

(A) <u>대부분의 사람들은 아침이든 저녁이든 혹은 오후든 간에 하루 중 그들이 자신의 최고의 상태에 있다고 느끼는 완벽한 시간을 갖는다.</u> Some of us are night owls, some early birds, and others in between may feel most active during the afternoon hours. If you are able to organize your day and divide your work, (B) **[deal / tasks / a point / time / the day / demand / of / your / with / that / make / it / attention / to / at / best].** However, if the task you face demands creativity and novel ideas, it's best to tackle it at your "worst" time of day! So if you are an early bird, make sure to attack your creative task in the evening, and vice versa for night owls. When your mind and body are less alert than at your "peak" hours, the muse of creativity awakens and is allowed to roam more freely. In other words, when your mental machinery is loose rather than standing at attention, the creativity flows.

*roam: (어슬렁어슬렁) 거닐다

---

46. 위 글의 밑줄 친 (A)의 우리말과 같도록 아래의 〈조건〉을 활용한 뒤 〈보기〉의 단어를 알맞게 영작하시오. 424)

〈조건〉
1. 관계부사를 사용할 것
2. 〈보기〉의 단어를 모두 사용하되, 필요시 변형 또는 추가하여 23단어로 쓸 것
(단, 동사는 기본형태이므로, 반드시 어형변화 해야 함)

〈보기〉
perfect / have / whether / feel / best / when

〈답〉

---

47. 위 글의 제목을 주어진 〈보기〉를 활용하여 서술하시오. 425)

〈보기〉
Task / during / Do / Worst / The / Time / To

〈답〉

---

48. 위 글의 밑줄 친 (B)에 주어진 단어를 활용하여 알맞게 영작하시오. 426)

〈답〉

2022년_고1_9월_인천광역시 교육청_학력평가_38번

Television is the number one leisure activity in the United States and Europe, consuming more than half of our free time. We generally think of television as a way to relax, tune out, and escape from our troubles for a bit each day. While this is true, there is increasing evidence that we are more motivated to tune in to our favorite shows and characters when we are feeling lonely or have a greater need for social connection. Television watching does satisfy these social needs to some extent, at least in the short run. Unfortunately, it is also likely to "crowd out" other activities that produce more sustainable social contributions to our social well-being. (A) 우리가 텔레비전을 더 볼수록, 우리는 사회적 관계망 속에서 우리의 시간을 기꺼이 할애하거나 사람들과 함께 시간을 덜 보내기 쉽다. In other words, (B) [for / make / friends / for / have / the / real / more / we / we / time / the / less / time / in / Friends, / life].

*Friends: 프렌즈(미국의 한 방송국에서 방영된 시트콤)

49. 위 글의 밑줄 친 (A)의 우리말과 같도록 아래의 <조건>을 활용한 뒤 <보기>의 단어를 알맞게 영작하시오.427)

―――――――――――― <조건> ――――――――――――
1. the 비교급 구문을 사용할 것
2. <보기>의 단어를 모두 사용하되, 필요시 변형 또는 추가하여 24단어로 쓸 것
(단, 동사는 기본형태이므로, 반드시 어형변화 해야 함)
―――――――――――― <보기> ――――――――――――
likely / spend / watch / less / volunteer / social

<답>

50. 위 글의 제목을 주어진 <보기>를 활용하여 서술하시오.428)

―――――――――――― <보기> ――――――――――――
Watching / The / Television / Trap / of

<답>

51. 위 글의 밑줄 친 (B)에 주어진 단어를 활용하여 알맞게 영작하시오.429)

<답>

2022년_고1_9월_인천광역시 교육청_학력평가_39번

(A) 우리는 종종 온도 개념을 우리가 물건을 만졌을 때 그것이 얼마나 뜨겁게 또는 차갑게 느껴지는지와 연관 짓는다. In this way, our senses provide us with a qualitative indication of temperature. Our senses, however, are unreliable and often mislead us. For example, if you stand in bare feet with one foot on carpet and the other on a tile floor, the tile feels colder than the carpet even though both are at the same temperature. The two objects feel different (B) [energy / tile / heat / at / than / by / rate / transfers / because / carpet / does / a higher]. Your skin "measures" the rate of energy transfer by heat rather than the actual temperature. What we need is a reliable and reproducible method for measuring the relative hotness or coldness of objects rather than the rate of energy transfer. Scientists have developed a variety of thermometers for making such quantitative measurements.

*thermometer: 온도계

52. 위 글의 밑줄 친 (A)의 우리말과 같도록 아래의 <조건>을 활용한 뒤 <보기>의 단어를 알맞게 영작하시오.430)

―――――――――――― <조건> ――――――――――――
1. 간접의문문을 사용할 것
2. <보기>의 단어를 모두 사용하되, 필요시 변형 또는 추가하여 19단어로 쓸 것
(단, 동사는 기본형태이므로, 반드시 어형변화 해야 함)
―――――――――――― <보기> ――――――――――――
touch / feel / associate / concept / often / how

<답>

53. 위 글의 제목을 주어진 <보기>를 활용하여 서술하시오.431)

―――――――――――― <보기> ――――――――――――
our / get / over / to / biases / how

<답>

54. 위 글의 밑줄 친 (B)에 주어진 단어를 활용하여 알맞게 영작하시오.432)

<답>

2022년_고1_9월_인천광역시 교육청_학력평가_40번

My colleagues and I ran an experiment testing two different messages meant to convince thousands of resistant alumni to make a donation. One message emphasized the opportunity to do good: donating would benefit students, faculty, and staff. The other emphasized the opportunity to feel good: donors would enjoy the warm glow of giving. The two messages were equally effective: in both cases, 6.5 percent of the unwilling alumni ended up donating. Then we combined them, because two reasons are better than one. Except they weren't. When we put the two reasons together, the giving rate dropped below 3 percent. (A) 각각의 이유가 단독으로는 그 두 개가 합쳐진 것보다 두 배 넘게 더 효과적이었다. The audience was already skeptical. When we gave them different kinds of reasons to donate, (B) [to / that / triggered / we / awareness / was / their / trying / they / it / shielded / persuade / themselves / someone / them — and / against].

* alumni: 졸업생 ** skeptical: 회의적인

↓

In the experiment mentioned above, when the two different reasons to donate were given simultaneously, the audience was less likely to be convinced because they could recognize the intention to persuade them.

---

55. 위 글의 밑줄 친 (A)의 우리말과 같도록 아래의 〈조건〉을 활용한 뒤 〈보기〉의 단어를 알맞게 영작하시오.433)

〈조건〉
1. 비교구문을 사용할 것   2. 〈보기〉의 단어를 모두 사용하되, 필요시 변형 또는 추가하여 13단어로 쓸 것   (단, 동사는 기본형태이므로, 반드시 어형변화 해야 함)
〈보기〉
effective / combine / twice / be / as
〈답〉

56. 위 글의 제목을 주어진 〈보기〉를 활용하여 서술하시오.434)

〈보기〉
A / A / of / When / Person / Convincing / Caution / Point
〈답〉

57. 위 글의 밑줄 친 (B)에 주어진 단어를 활용하여 알맞게 영작하시오.435)

〈답〉

2022년_고1_9월_인천광역시 교육청_학력평가_41~42번

In a society that rejects the consumption of insects there are some individuals who overcome this rejection, but most will continue with this attitude. It may be very difficult to convince an entire society that insects are totally suitable for consumption. (A) 하지만, 특정 음식에 대한 이러한 태도의 역전이 전체 사회에 발생해 온 사례들이 있다. Several examples in the past 120 years from European-American society are: considering lobster a luxury food instead of a food for servants and prisoners; considering sushi a safe and delicious food; and considering pizza not just a food for the rural poor of Sicily. In Latin American countries, where insects are already consumed, (B) [consumption / and / it / a portion / population / the / associates / hates / poverty / with / of / their]. There are also examples of people who have had the habit of consuming them and abandoned that habit due to shame, and because they do not want to be categorized as poor or uncivilized. According to Esther Katz, an anthropologist, if the consumption of insects as a food luxury is to be promoted, there would be more chances that some individuals who do not present this habit overcome ideas under which they were educated. And this could also help to revalue the consumption of insects by those people who already eat them.

58. 위 글의 밑줄 친 (A)의 우리말과 같도록 아래의 〈조건〉을 활용한 뒤 〈보기〉의 단어를 알맞게 영작하시오.436)

〈조건〉
1. 전치사 + 관계대명사 구조를 사용할 것
2. 〈보기〉의 단어를 모두 사용하되, 필요시 변형 또는 추가하여 19단어로 쓸 것
(단, 동사는 기본형태이므로, 반드시 어형변화 해야 함)

〈보기〉
happen / society / attitudes / entire / certain / reversal / which

〈답〉

59. 위 글의 제목을 주어진 〈보기〉를 활용하여 서술하시오.437)

〈보기〉
A / Attitude / toward / A / One's / Particular / Reversal / Food / of

〈답〉

60. 위 글의 밑줄 친 (B)에 주어진 단어를 활용하여 알맞게 영작하시오.438)

〈답〉

서술형 Lv_심화1

2022년_고1_9월_인천광역시 교육청_학력평가_18번

Dear Parents/Guardians, Class parties will be held on the afternoon December 16th, 2022. Children may bring in sweets, crisps, biscuits, cakes, and drinks. We are requesting that children do not bring in home-cooked or prepared food. (A) <u>모든 음식은 성분을 명확하게 목록으로 작성하여 밀봉된 꾸러미로 가져와야 합니다.</u> Fruit and vegetables are welcomed if they are pre-packed in a sealed packet from the shop. Please DO NOT send any food into school containing nuts as we have many children with severe nut allergies. (B) <u>아이들이 가져오는 모든 음식의 성분을 주의 깊게 확인해 주십시오.</u> Thank you for your continued support and cooperation. Yours sincerely, Lisa Brown, Headteacher

1. 위 글의 밑줄 친 (A)의 우리말과 같도록 아래의 〈조건〉을 활용한 뒤 〈보기〉의 단어를 알맞게 영작하시오.439)

〈조건〉
1. ① 과거분사를 활용할 것 ② with 분사구문을 활용할 것
2. 〈보기〉의 단어를 모두 사용하되, 필요시 변형 또는 추가하여 13단어로 쓸 것 (단, 동사는 기본형태이므로, 반드시 어형변화 해야 함)
〈보기〉
list / contain / severe / packet / arrive

〈답〉

2. 위 글의 주제를 주어진 〈보기〉를 활용하여 서술하시오.440)

〈보기〉
food / it / an / the / information / to / that / about / article / delivers / brought / class / the / parties / is

〈답〉

3. 위 글의 밑줄 친 (B)에 주어진 단어를 활용하여 알맞게 영작하시오.441)

〈보기〉
bring / check / ingredients / food / carefully / please / of / children / the / all / your

〈답〉

2022년_고1_9월_인천광역시 교육청_학력평가_19번

It was two hours before the submission deadline and I still hadn't finished my news article. I sat at the desk, but suddenly, the typewriter didn't work. (A) <u>내가 아무리 세게 키를 두드려도, 레버는 종이를 두드리려 움직이지 않았다.</u> I started to realize that I would not be able to finish the article on time. (B) <u>필사적으로, 나는 타자기를 내 무릎 위에 올려놓고 각각의 키를 내가 할 수 있을 만큼의 많은 힘을 가지고 누르기 시작했다.</u> Nothing happened. Thinking something might have happened inside of it, I opened the cover, lifted up the keys, and found the problem — a paper clip. The keys had no room to move. After picking it out, I pressed and pulled some parts. The keys moved smoothly again. I breathed deeply and smiled. Now I knew that I could finish my article on time.

4. 위 글의 밑줄 친 (A)의 우리말과 같도록 아래의 〈조건〉을 활용한 뒤 〈보기〉의 단어를 알맞게 영작하시오.442)

〈조건〉
1. ① no matter ~ 구문을 활용할 것
2. 〈보기〉의 단어를 모두 사용하되, 필요시 변형 또는 추가하여 16단어로 쓸 것 (단, 동사는 기본형태이므로, 반드시 어형변화 해야 함)
〈보기〉
matter / hard / tap / strike / lever / paper / move

〈답〉

5. 위 글의 주제를 주어진 〈보기〉를 활용하여 서술하시오.443)

〈보기〉
the / down / broke / for / the / a / while / because / clip / of / typewriter / paper

〈답〉

6. 위 글의 밑줄 친 (B)에 주어진 단어를 활용하여 알맞게 영작하시오.444)

〈보기〉
hitting / much / the typewriter / force / with / each / as / started / I / key / I / on / my / could / desperately, / manage. / as / rested / and / lap

〈답〉

2022년_고1_9월_인천광역시 교육청_학력평가_20번

Experts on writing say, "Get rid of as many words as possible." Each word must do something important. If it doesn't, get rid of it. Well, this doesn't work for speaking. (B) <u>말을 할 때는 아이디어를 소개하고, 표현하며, 적절히 부연 설명하는 데 글을 쓸 때보다 더 많은 단어가 필요하다.</u> Why is this so? While the reader can reread, the listener cannot rehear. Speakers do not come equipped with a replay button. Because listeners are easily distracted, they will miss many pieces of what a speaker says. If they miss the crucial sentence, they may never catch up. (A) <u>이것은 화자들이 그들의 요점에 대해 더 길게 말할 필요가 있게 한다</u>, using more words on them than would be used to express the same idea in writing.

7. 위 글의 밑줄 친 (A)의 우리말과 같도록 아래의 〈조건〉을 활용한 뒤 〈보기〉의 단어를 알맞게 영작하시오.445)

〈조건〉
1. ① 가목적어 진목적어 구문을 활용할 것 ② 의미상 주어를 활용할 것
2. 〈보기〉의 단어를 모두 사용하되, 필요시 변형 또는 추가하여 12단어로 쓸 것
(단, 동사는 기본형태이므로, 반드시 어형변화 해야 함)

〈보기〉
necessary / long / speaker / make / point

〈답〉

8. 위 글의 주제를 주어진 〈보기〉를 활용하여 서술하시오.446)

〈보기〉
writing, / words / speaking / be / in / used / more / unlike / should

〈답〉

9. 위 글의 밑줄 친 (B)에 주어진 단어를 활용하여 알맞게 영작하시오.447)

〈보기〉
it / introduce, / speech / / to / in / takes / elaborate / in / more / words / express, and / writing. / an idea / than / adequately / it / takes

〈답〉

2022년_고1_9월_인천광역시 교육청_학력평가_21번

Is the customer always right? When customers return a broken product to a famous company, which makes kitchen and bathroom fixtures, the company nearly always offers a replacement to maintain good customer relations. Still, "there are times you've got to say 'no,'" explains the warranty expert of the company, (A) <u>그 회사의 상품 보증 전문가는 상품이 멀쩡하거나 남용되었을 때와 같이.</u> Entrepreneur Lauren Thorp, who owns an e-commerce company, says, "While the customer is 'always' right, sometimes you just have to fire a customer." When Thorp has tried everything to resolve a complaint and realizes that the customer will be dissatisfied no matter what, (B) <u>그녀는 자신의 주의를 나머지 다른 고객들에게 돌리는데, 그 고객들은 "내 성공의 이유"라고 그녀는 말한다.</u>

10. 위 글의 밑줄 친 (A)의 우리말과 같도록 아래의 〈조건〉을 활용한 뒤 〈보기〉의 단어를 알맞게 영작하시오.448)

〈조건〉
1. ① 수동태를 활용할 것 ② 현재완료 수동태를 활용할 것
2. 〈보기〉의 단어를 모두 사용하되, 필요시 변형 또는 추가하여 11단어로 쓸 것
(단, 동사는 기본형태이므로, 반드시 어형변화 해야 함)

〈보기〉
abuse / product / undamage / such

〈답〉

11. 위 글의 주제를 주어진 〈보기〉를 활용하여 서술하시오.449)

〈보기〉
there / should / the / the / sometimes / reject / request / company / be / times / customer's / when

〈답〉

12. 위 글의 밑줄 친 (B)에 주어진 단어를 활용하여 알맞게 영작하시오.450)

〈보기〉
says / to / she / her / her / customers, / who / of / "the reason for my success." / she / returns / the / rest / are / attention

〈답〉

스승의날
Teachers Day Publisher

2022년_고1_9월_인천광역시 교육청_학력평가_22번

A recent study from Carnegie Mellon University in Pittsburgh, called "When Too Much of a Good Thing May Be Bad," indicates that classrooms with too much decoration are a source of distraction for young children and directly affect their cognitive performance. (B) 시각적으로 지나치게 자극되었을 때, 아이들은 집중하는 데 많이 어려워하고 결국 더 나쁜 학습 결과로 끝이 난다. On the other hand, if there is not much decoration on the classroom walls, (A) 아이들은 덜 산만해지고, 그들의 활동에 더 많은 시간을 사용하고, 더 많이 배운다. So it's our job, in order to support their attention, to find the right balance between excessive decoration and the complete absence of it.

13. 위 글의 밑줄 친 (A)의 우리말과 같도록 아래의 〈조건〉을 활용한 뒤 〈보기〉의 단어를 알맞게 영작하시오.451)

〈조건〉
1. ① 병렬구조를 활용할 것 ② 비교급을 활용할 것
2. 〈보기〉의 단어를 모두 사용하되, 필요시 변형 또는 추가하여 14단어로 쓸 것
(단, 동사는 기본형태이므로, 반드시 어형변화 해야 함)

〈보기〉
children / distract / learn / time / activity / spend

〈답〉

14. 위 글의 주제를 주어진 〈보기〉를 활용하여 서술하시오.452)

〈보기〉
classroom / be / should / utilized / that / decorations / appropriately / affect / learning / children's

〈답〉

15. 위 글의 밑줄 친 (B)에 주어진 단어를 활용하여 알맞게 영작하시오.453)

〈보기〉
overstimulated, / have / results. / up / with / a great / visually / and / end / worse / children / the / being / concentrating / academic / difficulty / deal / of

〈답〉

2022년_고1_9월_인천광역시 교육청_학력평가_23번

For creatures like us, evolution smiled upon those with a strong need to belong. Survival and reproduction are the criteria of success by natural selection, and forming relationships with other people can be useful for both survival and reproduction. Groups can share resources, care for sick members, scare off predators, fight together against enemies, (B) 효율성을 향상시키기 위해 일을 나누고, 많은 다른 방식에서 생존에 기여한다. In particular, if an individual and a group want the same resource, the group will generally prevail, (A) 그래서 자원에 대한 경쟁은 소속하려는 욕구를 특별히 좋아할 것이다. Belongingness will likewise promote reproduction, such as by bringing potential mates into contact with each other, and in particular by keeping parents together to care for their children, who are much more likely to survive if they have more than one caregiver.

16. 위 글의 밑줄 친 (A)의 우리말과 같도록 아래의 〈조건〉을 활용한 뒤 〈보기〉의 단어를 알맞게 영작하시오.454)

〈조건〉
1. ① to 부정사를 활용할 것
2. 〈보기〉의 단어를 모두 사용하되, 필요시 변형 또는 추가하여 11단어로 쓸 것
(단, 동사는 기본형태이므로, 반드시 어형변화 해야 함)

〈보기〉
favor / resource / especially / competition / belong / need

〈답〉

17. 위 글의 주제를 주어진 〈보기〉를 활용하여 서술하시오.455)

〈보기〉
evolution / is / useful / belonging / for / human

〈답〉

18. 위 글의 밑줄 친 (B)에 주어진 단어를 활용하여 알맞게 영작하시오.456)

〈보기〉
to / and / as / efficiency, / improve / tasks / many / other / divide / / survival / ways. / in / to / contribute / so

〈답〉

2022년_고1_9월_인천광역시 교육청_학력평가_24번

Many people make a mistake of only operating along the safe zones, and in the process they miss the opportunity to achieve greater things. They do so because of a fear of the unknown and a fear of treading the unknown paths of life. Those that are brave enough to take those roads less travelled are able to get great returns and derive major satisfaction out of their courageous moves. Being overcautious will mean that you will miss attaining the greatest levels of your potential. (A) <u>여러분은 주변에 있는 많은 사람들이 선택하지 않을 기회를 택하는 것을 배워야 한다.</u> because (B) <u>여러분의 성공은 삶의 과정에서 여러분이 내릴 용감한 결정으로부터 나올 것이다.</u>

19. 위 글의 밑줄 친 (A)의 우리말과 같도록 아래의 〈조건〉을 활용한 뒤 〈보기〉의 단어를 알맞게 영작하시오.457)

〈조건〉
1. ① to 부정사를 활용할 것 ② 관계대명사를 활용할 것
2. 〈보기〉의 단어를 모두 사용하되, 필요시 변형 또는 추가하여 15단어로 쓸 것
(단, 동사는 기본형태이므로, 반드시 어형변화 해야 함)

〈보기〉
learn / chance / take / must / those / that

〈답〉

20. 위 글의 주제를 주어진 〈보기〉를 활용하여 서술하시오.458)

〈보기〉
decisions / the / comes / brave / of / course / in / life / from / success

〈답〉

21. 위 글의 밑줄 친 (B)에 주어진 단어를 활용하여 알맞게 영작하시오.459)

〈보기〉
will / bold / flow / you / that / decisions / along / will / success / way / from / the / take / your / those

〈답〉

2022년_고1_9월_인천광역시 교육청_학력평가_29번

The human brain, it turns out, has shrunk in mass by about 10 percent since it peaked in size 15,000-30,000 years ago. One possible reason is that many thousands of years ago humans lived in a world of dangerous predators where they had to have their wits about them at all times to avoid being killed. Today, we have effectively domesticated ourselves and many of the tasks of survival — from avoiding immediate death to building shelters to obtaining food — have been outsourced to the wider society. We are smaller than our ancestors too, and (A) <u>가축이 그들의 야생 사촌보다 일반적으로 더 작다는 것은 가축의 한 특징이다.</u> None of this may mean we are dumber — __brain size is not necessarily an indicator of human intelligence — (B) <u>그것은 오늘날 우리의 뇌가 다르게 타고났다는 것을 의미할지도 모른다.</u>, and perhaps more efficiently, than those of our ancestors.

22. 위 글의 밑줄 친 (A)의 우리말과 같도록 아래의 〈조건〉을 활용한 뒤 〈보기〉의 단어를 알맞게 영작하시오.460)

〈조건〉
1. ① 가주어 진주어 구문을 활용할 것 ② 비교구문을 활용할 것
2. 〈보기〉의 단어를 모두 사용하되, 필요시 변형 또는 추가하여 16단어로 쓸 것
(단, 동사는 기본형태이므로, 반드시 어형변화 해야 함)

〈보기〉
cousin / domestic / characteristic / animal

〈답〉

23. 위 글의 주제를 주어진 〈보기〉를 활용하여 서술하시오.461)

〈보기〉
smaller / than / are / past / in / brains / our / the

〈답〉

24. 위 글의 밑줄 친 (B)에 주어진 단어를 활용하여 알맞게 영작하시오.462)

〈보기〉
differently / that / it / wired / are / up / brains / today / may / but / our / mean

〈답〉

2022년_고1_9월_인천광역시 교육청_학력평가_30번

It is widely believed that certain herbs somehow magically improve the work of certain organs, and "cure" specific diseases as a result. Such statements are unscientific and groundless. Sometimes herbs appear to work, since they tend to increase your blood circulation in an aggressive attempt by your body to eliminate them from your system. That can create a temporary feeling of a high, which makes it seem as if your health condition has improved. Also, herbs can have a placebo effect, just like any other method, thus helping you feel better. (A) 어떠한 경우든, 건강을 되찾게 하는 지성을 가진 것은 허브가 아니라 바로 당신의 몸이다. How can herbs have the intelligence needed to direct your body into getting healthier? That is impossible. Try to imagine (B) 어떻게 허브가 당신의 몸 안으로 들어가 영리하게 당신의 문제를 해결할 수 있는지를. If you try to do that, you will see how impossible it seems. Otherwise, it would mean that herbs are more intelligent than the human body, which is truly hard to believe.

*placebo effect: 위약 효과

25. 위 글의 밑줄 친 (A)의 우리말과 같도록 아래의 〈조건〉을 활용한 뒤 〈보기〉의 단어를 알맞게 영작하시오.463)

〈조건〉
1. ① it that 강조구문을 활용할 것 ② to 부정사를 활용할 것
2. 〈보기〉의 단어를 모두 사용하되, 필요시 변형 또는 추가하여 18단어로 쓸 것
(단, 동사는 기본형태이므로, 반드시 어형변화 해야 함)

〈보기〉
herb / regain / whatever / intelligence / body

〈답〉

26. 위 글의 주제를 주어진 〈보기〉를 활용하여 서술하시오.464)

〈보기〉
don't / us / make / healthier / herbs

〈답〉

27. 위 글의 밑줄 친 (B)에 주어진 단어를 활용하여 알맞게 영작하시오.465)

〈보기〉
might / come / and / into / body / fix / intelligently / problems / herbs / your / how / your

〈답〉

2022년_고1_9월_인천광역시 교육청_학력평가_31번

We worry that the robots are taking our jobs, but just as common a problem is that the robots are taking our judgment. In the large warehouses so common behind the scenes of today's economy, human 'pickers' hurry around grabbing products off shelves and moving them to where they can be packed and dispatched. In their ears are headpieces: the voice of 'Jennifer', a piece of software, (A) 그들의 움직임의 가장 작은 세부 사항들을 조종하면서, 그들에게 어디로 갈지와 무엇을 할지를 말한다. Jennifer breaks down instructions into tiny chunks, to minimise error and maximise productivity — for example, rather than picking eighteen copies of a book off a shelf, the human worker would be politely instructed to pick five. Then another five. Then yet another five. Then another three. Working in such conditions reduces people to machines made of flesh. (B) 우리에게 생각하거나 적응하라고 요구하기보다는, the Jennifer unit takes over the thought process and treats workers as an inexpensive source of some visual processing and a pair of opposable thumbs.

*dispatch: 발송하다 **chunk: 덩어리

28. 위 글의 밑줄 친 (A)의 우리말과 같도록 아래의 〈조건〉을 활용한 뒤 〈보기〉의 단어를 알맞게 영작하시오.466)

〈조건〉
1. ① 의문사 to 부정사 구문을 활용할 것 ② 분사구문을 활용할 것
2. 〈보기〉의 단어를 모두 사용하되, 필요시 변형 또는 추가하여 16단어로 쓸 것
(단, 동사는 기본형태이므로, 반드시 어형변화 해야 함)

〈보기〉
detail / control / movement / where / tell / what

〈답〉

29. 위 글의 주제를 주어진 〈보기〉를 활용하여 서술하시오.467)

〈보기〉
human / robots / away / taking / judgment / are

〈답〉

30. 위 글의 밑줄 친 (B)에 주어진 단어를 활용하여 알맞게 영작하시오.468)

〈보기〉
think / asking / rather / or / than / to / us / adapt

〈답〉

2022년_고1_9월_인천광역시 교육청_학력평가_32번

The prevailing view among developmental scientists is that people are active contributors to their own development. (A) <u>사람들은 그들이 사는 물리적인 그리고 사회적인 환경의 영향을 받지만,</u> but they also play a role in influencing their development by interacting with, and changing, those contexts. Even infants influence the world around them and construct their own development through their interactions. Consider an infant who smiles at each adult he sees; he influences his world because adults are likely to smile, use "baby talk," and play with him in response. The infant brings adults into close contact, making one-on-one interactions and creating opportunities for learning. (B) <u>그들 주변 세상의 관심을 끌고, 생각하고, 호기심을 가지고, 그리고 그들 주변의 사람들, 사물들, 그리고 세상과 상호 작용함으로써,</u> individuals of all ages are "manufacturers of their own development."

31. 위 글의 밑줄 친 (A)의 우리말과 같도록 아래의 <조건>을 활용한 뒤 <보기>의 단어를 알맞게 영작하시오.469)

<조건>
1. ① 수동태를 활용할 것 ② 전치사 + 관계대명사 구조를 활용할 것
2. <보기>의 단어를 모두 사용하되, 필요시 변형 또는 추가하여 13단어로 쓸 것
(단, 동사는 기본형태이므로, 반드시 어형변화 해야 함)

<보기>
context / physical / influence / social / live

<답>

32. 위 글의 주제를 주어진 <보기>를 활용하여 서술하시오.470)

<보기>
development / actively / their / people / contribute / own

<답>

33. 위 글의 밑줄 친 (B)에 주어진 단어를 활용하여 알맞게 영작하시오.471)

<보기>
curious, and / around / people, / thinking, / them / engaging / interacting / the world / objects, and / around / by / with / them, / being / the world

<답>

2022년_고1_9월_인천광역시 교육청_학력평가_33번

The demand for freshness can have hidden environmental costs. While freshness is now being used as a term in food marketing as part of a return to nature, the demand for year-round supplies of fresh produce such as soft fruit and exotic vegetables has led to the widespread use of hot houses in cold climates and increasing reliance on total quality control — management by temperature control, use of pesticides and computer/satellite-based logistics. The demand for freshness has also contributed to concerns about food wastage. Use of 'best before', 'sell by' and 'eat by' labels (A) <u>제도적인 폐기물 생산을 법적으로 허용해 왔다.</u> Campaigners have exposed the scandal of overproduction and waste. Tristram Stuart, one of the global band of anti-waste campaigners, argues that, (B) <u>신선하게 만들어진 샌드위치와 함께,</u> over-ordering is standard practice across the retail sector to avoid the appearance of empty shelf space, leading to high volumes of waste when supply regularly exceeds demand.

* pesticide: 살충제 ** logistics: 물류, 유통

34. 위 글의 밑줄 친 (A)의 우리말과 같도록 아래의 <조건>을 활용한 뒤 <보기>의 단어를 알맞게 영작하시오.472)

<조건>
1. ① 현재완료를 활용할 것
2. <보기>의 단어를 모두 사용하되, 필요시 변형 또는 추가하여 5단어로 쓸 것
(단, 동사는 기본형태이므로, 반드시 어형변화 해야 함)

<보기>
institutional / legally / allow

<답>

35. 위 글의 주제를 주어진 <보기>를 활용하여 서술하시오.473)

<보기>
has / a / freshness / for / demand / the / variety / environmental / of / costs

<답>

36. 위 글의 밑줄 친 (B)에 주어진 단어를 활용하여 알맞게 영작하시오.474)

<보기>
sandwiches / freshly / made / with

<답>

2022년_고1_9월_인천광역시 교육청_학력평가_34번

In the studies of Colin Cherry at the Massachusetts Institute for Technology back in the 1950s, his participants listened to voices in one ear at a time and then through both ears in an effort (A) <u>우리가 두 사람이 이야기하는 것을 동시에 들을 수 있는지 판단하기 위해</u> One ear always contained a message that the listener had to repeat back (called "shadowing") while the other ear included people speaking. The trick was to see if you could totally focus on the main message and also hear someone talking in your other ear. Cleverly, Cherry (B) <u>참가자들이 다른 한쪽 귀로 들리는 메시지가 남자가 말한 것인지 혹은 여자가 말한 것인지, 영어인지 다른 외국어인지, 심지어 실제 단어로 구성된 것인지조차 알아차리기가 전혀 가능하지 않다는 것을 발견했다.</u> In other words, people could not process two pieces of information at the same time.

37. 위 글의 밑줄 친 (A)의 우리말과 같도록 아래의 〈조건〉을 활용한 뒤 〈보기〉의 단어를 알맞게 영작하시오. 475)

〈조건〉

1. ① 지각동사 구문을 활용할 것
2. 〈보기〉의 단어를 모두 사용하되, 필요시 변형 또는 추가하여 14단어로 쓸 것
(단, 동사는 기본형태이므로, 반드시 어형변화 해야 함)

〈보기〉

determine / whether / same / listen / talk

〈답〉

38. 위 글의 주제를 주어진 〈보기〉를 활용하여 서술하시오. 476)

〈보기〉

two / at / the / process / people / pieces / information / of / same / time / cannot

〈답〉

39. 위 글의 밑줄 친 (B)에 주어진 단어를 활용하여 알맞게 영작하시오. 477)

〈보기〉

English / another / found / it / words / language, / at / in / whether / woman, / or / was / the / in / his / or / was / of / for / a man / know / participants / the message / by / even / other / or / to / comprised / real / spoken / impossible / was / ear / all

〈답〉

2022년_고1_9월_인천광역시 교육청_학력평가_35번

The fast-paced evolution of Information and Communication Technologies (ICTs) has radically transformed the dynamics and business models of the tourism and hospitality industry. This leads to new levels/forms of competitiveness among service providers and transforms the customer experience through new services. Creating unique experiences and providing convenient services to customers leads to satisfaction and, eventually, customer loyalty to the service provider or brand (i.e., hotels). In particular, (B) <u>관광업 분야에서 받아들여진 가장 최근의 상승은 모바일 애플리케이션에 의해 대표된다.</u> Indeed, (A) <u>관광객에게 호텔 예약, 항공권 발권, 그리고 지역 관광지를 추천하는 것과 같은 서비스에 대한 모바일 접근 권한을 주는 것은 강력한 흥미와 상당한 수익을 만들어 낸다.</u>

 * hospitality industry: 서비스업(호텔·식당업 등)

40. 위 글의 밑줄 친 (A)의 우리말과 같도록 아래의 〈조건〉을 활용한 뒤 〈보기〉의 단어를 알맞게 영작하시오. 478)

〈조건〉

1. ① 동명사를 활용할 것 ② 병렬구조를 활용할 것
2. 〈보기〉의 단어를 모두 사용하되, 필요시 변형 또는 추가하여 24단어로 쓸 것
(단, 동사는 기본형태이므로, 반드시 어형변화 해야 함)

〈보기〉

ticketing / service / considerable / empower / reservation / access / attraction / generate / local

〈답〉

41. 위 글의 주제를 주어진 〈보기〉를 활용하여 서술하시오. 479)

〈보기〉

industries / information / communication / tourism / changed / the / dynamically / and / technologies / has / hospitality / andl

〈답〉

42. 위 글의 밑줄 친 (B)에 주어진 단어를 활용하여 알맞게 영작하시오. 480)

〈보기〉

is / by / the tourism / applications / sector / boost / the / technological / received / represented / most / mobile / by / recent

〈답〉

스승의날 영어연구소

With nearly a billion hungry people in the world, there is obviously no single cause. However, far and away the biggest cause is poverty. Seventy-nine percent of the world's hungry (B) 식량 순 수출국에 살고 있다. How can this be? The reason people are hungry in those countries is that the products produced there can be sold on the world market for more than the local citizens can afford to pay for them. In the modern age you do not starve because you have no food, you starve because you have no money. So the problem really is that food is, in the grand scheme of things, too expensive and (A) 많은 사람들은 너무 가난하여 그것을 구매할 수 없다는 것이다. The answer will be in continuing the trend of lowering the cost of food.

* net exporter: 순 수출국 ** scheme: 체계, 조직

43. 위 글의 밑줄 친 (A)의 우리말과 같도록 아래의 〈조건〉을 활용한 뒤 〈보기〉의 단어를 알맞게 영작하시오.481)

〈조건〉
1. ① too ~ to ... 구문을 활용할 것
2. 〈보기〉의 단어를 모두 사용하되, 필요시 변형 또는 추가하여 8단어로 쓸 것
(단, 동사는 기본형태이므로, 반드시 어형변화 해야 함)

〈보기〉
many / poor / people / buy

〈답〉

44. 위 글의 주제를 주어진 〈보기〉를 활용하여 서술하시오.482)

〈보기〉
because / have / don't / than / hungry / people / go / money / other / food / they

〈답〉

45. 위 글의 밑줄 친 (B)에 주어진 단어를 활용하여 알맞게 영작하시오.483)

〈보기〉
of / nations / are / food / net / in / that / live / exporters

〈답〉

Most people have a perfect time of day (A) 그들이 자신의 최고의 상태에 있다고 느끼는, whether in the morning, evening, or afternoon. Some of us are night owls, some early birds, and others in between may feel most active during the afternoon hours. If you are able to organize your day and divide your work, make it a point to deal with tasks that demand attention at your best time of the day. However, if the task you face demands creativity and novel ideas, it's best to tackle it at your "worst" time of day! So if you are an early bird, make sure to attack your creative task in the evening, and vice versa for night owls. When your mind and body are less alert than at your "peak" hours, (B) 창의성의 영감이 깨어나 더 자유롭게 거니는 것이 허용된다. In other words, when your mental machinery is loose rather than standing at attention, the creativity flows.

*roam: (어슬렁어슬렁) 거닐다

46. 위 글의 밑줄 친 (A)의 우리말과 같도록 아래의 〈조건〉을 활용한 뒤 〈보기〉의 단어를 알맞게 영작하시오.484)

〈조건〉
1. ① 관계부사를 활용할 것
2. 〈보기〉의 단어를 모두 사용하되, 필요시 변형 또는 추가하여 8단어로 쓸 것
(단, 동사는 기본형태이므로, 반드시 어형변화 해야 함)

〈보기〉
feel / best / they

〈답〉

47. 위 글의 주제를 주어진 〈보기〉를 활용하여 서술하시오.485)

〈보기〉
to / perform / is / the / it / good / new / that / require / creativity / and / individual / tasks / at / worst / time / of / ideas / an

〈답〉

48. 위 글의 밑줄 친 (B)에 주어진 단어를 활용하여 알맞게 영작하시오.486)

〈보기〉
more / freely / to / awakens / creativity / allowed / and / roam / the muse / is / of

〈답〉

Television is the number one leisure activity in the United States and Europe, consuming more than half of our free time. We generally think of television as a way to relax, tune out, and escape from our troubles for a bit each day. While this is true, there is increasing evidence that we are more motivated to tune in to our favorite shows and characters when we are feeling lonely or have a greater need for social connection. Television watching does satisfy these social needs to some extent, at least in the short run. Unfortunately, it is also likely to "crowd out" other activities that produce more sustainable social contributions to our social well-being. (A) <u>우리가 텔레비전을 더 볼수록, 우리는 사회적 관계망 속에서 우리의 시간을 기꺼이 할애하거나 사람들과 함께 시간을 덜 보내기 쉽다.</u> In other words, (B) <u>우리가 Friends를 위해 더 많은 시간을 낼수록, 실제 친구들을 위해서는 시간을 덜 갖게 된다.</u>

*Friends: 프렌즈(미국의 한 방송국에서 방영된 시트콤)

49. 위 글의 밑줄 친 (A)의 우리말과 같도록 아래의 〈조건〉을 활용한 뒤 〈보기〉의 단어를 알맞게 영작하시오.487)

〈조건〉
1. ① the 비교급 구문을 활용할 것 ② 병렬구조를 활용할 것
2. 〈보기〉의 단어를 모두 사용하되, 필요시 변형 또는 추가하여 24단어로 쓸 것
(단, 동사는 기본형태이므로, 반드시 어형변화 해야 함)

〈보기〉
television / volunteer / spend / network / social / watch / likely

〈답〉

50. 위 글의 주제를 주어진 〈보기〉를 활용하여 서술하시오.488)

〈보기〉
for / watching / to / is / our / easy / well-being / television / limit / activities / social

〈답〉

51. 위 글의 밑줄 친 (B)에 주어진 단어를 활용하여 알맞게 영작하시오.489)

〈보기〉
for / make / friends / for / have / the / real / more / we / we / time / the / less / time / in / Friends, / life

〈답〉

(A) <u>우리는 종종 온도 개념을 우리가 물건을 만졌을 때 그것이 얼마나 뜨겁게 또는 차갑게 느껴지는지와 연관 짓는다.</u> In this way, our senses provide us with a qualitative indication of temperature. Our senses, however, are unreliable and often mislead us. For example, if you stand in bare feet with one foot on carpet and the other on a tile floor, the tile feels colder than the carpet even though both are at the same temperature. The two objects feel different (B) <u>타일이 카페트가 전달하는 것보다 더 높은 비율로 에너지를 열의 형태로 전달하기 때문에.</u> Your skin "measures" the rate of energy transfer by heat rather than the actual temperature. What we need is a reliable and reproducible method for measuring the relative hotness or coldness of objects rather than the rate of energy transfer. Scientists have developed a variety of thermometers for making such quantitative measurements.

*thermometer: 온도계

52. 위 글의 밑줄 친 (A)의 우리말과 같도록 아래의 〈조건〉을 활용한 뒤 〈보기〉의 단어를 알맞게 영작하시오.490)

〈조건〉
1. ① 간접의문문을 활용할 것
2. 〈보기〉의 단어를 모두 사용하되, 필요시 변형 또는 추가하여 19단어로 쓸 것
(단, 동사는 기본형태이므로, 반드시 어형변화 해야 함)

〈보기〉
associate / concept / object / feel / how / touch

〈답〉

53. 위 글의 주제를 주어진 〈보기〉를 활용하여 서술하시오.491)

〈보기〉
the / rate / by / transfer / not / of / energy / heat, / skin / actual / temperature / our / measures

〈답〉

54. 위 글의 밑줄 친 (B)에 주어진 단어를 활용하여 알맞게 영작하시오.492)

〈보기〉
energy / tile / heat / at / than / by / rate / transfers / because / carpet / does / a higher

〈답〉

2022년_고1_9월_인천광역시 교육청_학력평가_40번

My colleagues and I ran an experiment testing two different messages meant to convince thousands of resistant alumni to make a donation. One message emphasized the opportunity to do good: donating would benefit students, faculty, and staff. The other emphasized the opportunity to feel good: donors would enjoy the warm glow of giving. The two messages were equally effective: in both cases, 6.5 percent of the unwilling alumni ended up donating. Then we combined them, because two reasons are better than one. Except they weren't. When we put the two reasons together, the giving rate dropped below 3 percent. (A) 각각의 이유가 단독으로는 그 두 개가 합쳐진 것보다 두 배 넘게 더 효과적이었다. The audience was already skeptical. When we gave them different kinds of reasons to donate, (B) 우리는 누군가가 그들을 설득하려고 하는 중이라는 그들의 인식을 유발했고 — 그리고 그들은 그것에 맞서 스스로를 보호했다.

* alumni: 졸업생 ** skeptical: 회의적인

↓

 In the experiment mentioned above, when the two different reasons to donate were given simultaneously, the audience was less likely to be convinced because they could recognize the intention to persuade them.

55. 위 글의 밑줄 친 (A)의 우리말과 같도록 아래의 〈조건〉을 활용한 뒤 〈보기〉의 단어를 알맞게 영작하시오.493)

〈조건〉
1. ① 비교구문을 활용할 것 ② 과거분사를 활용할 것
2. 〈보기〉의 단어를 모두 사용하되, 필요시 변형 또는 추가하여 13단어로 쓸 것
(단, 동사는 기본형태이므로, 반드시 어형변화 해야 함)

〈보기〉
effective / reason / combine / twice

〈답〉

56. 위 글의 주제를 주어진 〈보기〉를 활용하여 서술하시오.494)

〈보기〉
intentions / when / be / it / harder / the / people / find / notice / persuade / to / them / they / to / convinced

〈답〉

57. 위 글의 밑줄 친 (B)에 주어진 단어를 활용하여 알맞게 영작하시오.495)

〈보기〉
to / that / triggered / we / awareness / was / their / trying / they / it / shielded / persuade / themselves / someone / them — and / against

〈답〉

2022년_고1_9월_인천광역시 교육청_학력평가_41~42번

In a society that rejects the consumption of insects there are some individuals who overcome this rejection, but most will continue with this attitude. It may be very difficult to convince an entire society that insects are totally suitable for consumption. (A) 하지만, 특정 음식에 대한 이러한 태도의 역전이 전체 사회에 발생해 온 사례들이 있다. Several examples in the past 120 years from European-American society are: considering lobster a luxury food instead of a food for servants and prisoners; considering sushi a safe and delicious food; and considering pizza not just a food for the rural poor of Sicily. In Latin American countries, where insects are already consumed, (B) 인구의 일부는 그들의 섭취를 싫어하고 그것을 빈곤과 연관 짓는다. There are also examples of people who have had the habit of consuming them and abandoned that habit due to shame, and because they do not want to be categorized as poor or uncivilized. According to Esther Katz, an anthropologist, if the consumption of insects as a food luxury is to be promoted, there would be more chances that some individuals who do not present this habit overcome ideas under which they were educated. And this could also help to revalue the consumption of insects by those people who already eat them.

58. 위 글의 밑줄 친 (A)의 우리말과 같도록 아래의 〈조건〉을 활용한 뒤 〈보기〉의 단어를 알맞게 영작하시오.496)

〈조건〉

1. ① 전치사 + 관계대명사 구조를 활용할 것
   ② 현재완료를 활용할 것
2. 〈보기〉의 단어를 모두 사용하되, 필요시 변형 또는 추가하여 19단어로 쓸 것
   (단, 동사는 기본형태이므로, 반드시 어형변화 해야 함)

〈보기〉

happen / example / entire / reversal / attitude / society

〈답〉

59. 위 글의 주제를 주어진 〈보기〉를 활용하여 서술하시오.497)

〈보기〉

it / and / foods, / to / effects / is / society / attitude / toward / reverse / but / throughout / certain / occurs / difficult / it / the / has / many / also

〈답〉

60. 위 글의 밑줄 친 (B)에 주어진 단어를 활용하여 알맞게 영작하시오.498)

〈보기〉

consumption / and / it / a portion / population / the / associates / hates / poverty / with / of / their

〈답〉

서술형 Lv_심화2

2022년_고1_9월_인천광역시 교육청_학력평가_18번

Dear Parents/Guardians, Class parties will be held on the afternoon December 16th, 2022. Children may bring in sweets, crisps, biscuits, cakes, and drinks. We are requesting that children do not bring in home-cooked or prepared food. (1)_____

_____. Fruit and vegetables are welcomed if they are pre-packed in a sealed packet from the shop. (2)_____

_____. (3)_____

_____. Thank you for your continued support and cooperation. Yours sincerely, Lisa Brown, Headteacher

1. 위 글의 밑줄 친 부분을 영작하시오. 499)

〈답〉

2. 위 글의 밑줄 친 부분을 영작하시오. 500)

〈답〉

3. 위 글의 밑줄 친 부분을 영작하시오. 501)

〈답〉

4. 위 지문을 참고하여 다음 요약문을 완성하시오. 502)

〈요약〉 The letter outlines several _____and requests on the food that children _____ bring to the class party.

2022년_고1_9월_인천광역시 교육청_학력평가_20번

Experts on writing say, "Get rid of as many words as possible." Each word must do something important. If it doesn't, get rid of it. Well, this doesn't work for speaking. (1)_____

_____. Why is this so? While the reader can reread, the listener cannot rehear. Speakers do not come equipped with a replay button. Because listeners are easily distracted, they will miss many pieces of what a speaker says. If they miss the crucial sentence, they may never catch up. (2)_____

_____, (3)_____

_____

5. 위 글의 밑줄 친 부분을 영작하시오. 503)

〈답〉

6. 위 글의 밑줄 친 부분을 영작하시오. 504)

〈답〉

7. 위 글의 밑줄 친 부분을 영작하시오. 505)

〈답〉

8. 위 지문을 참고하여 다음 요약문을 완성하시오. 506)

〈요약〉 The passage on the difference between writing and _____explains why speech takes more _____to _____an idea than writing.

2022년_고1_9월_인천광역시 교육청_학력평가_21번

Is the customer always right? When customers return a broken product to a famous company, which makes kitchen and bathroom fixtures, the company nearly always offers a replacement to maintain good customer relations. (1)_____ _____ _____. Entrepreneur Lauren Thorp, who owns an e-commerce company, says, "While the customer is 'always' right, sometimes you just have to fire a customer." (2)_____ _____, (3)_____ _____

9. 위 글의 밑줄 친 부분을 영작하시오.507)

〈답〉

10. 위 글의 밑줄 친 부분을 영작하시오.508)

〈답〉

11. 위 글의 밑줄 친 부분을 영작하시오.509)

〈답〉

12. 위 지문을 참고하여 다음 요약문을 완성하시오.510)

〈요약〉 This passage that _____whether the customer is always right emphasizes that sometimes _____demand should be _____
.

2022년_고1_9월_인천광역시 교육청_학력평가_22번

A recent study from Carnegie Mellon University in Pittsburgh, called "When Too Much of a Good Thing May Be Bad," indicates that classrooms with too much decoration are a source of distraction for young children and directly affect their cognitive performance. (1)_____ _____. (2)_____ _____ _____. (3)_____ _____ _____.

13. 위 글의 밑줄 친 부분을 영작하시오.511)

〈답〉

14. 위 글의 밑줄 친 부분을 영작하시오.512)

〈답〉

15. 위 글의 밑줄 친 부분을 영작하시오.513)

〈답〉

16. 위 지문을 참고하여 다음 요약문을 완성하시오.514)

〈요약〉 _____a recent study from Carnegie Mellon University, the passage _____the importance of the _____amount of class decoration.

For creatures like us, evolution smiled upon those with a strong need to belong. Survival and reproduction are the criteria of success by natural selection, and forming relationships with other people can be useful for both survival and reproduction. (1)_____
_____
_____
_____. (2)_____
_____
_____. (3)_____
_____
_____
_____
_____

17. 위 글의 밑줄 친 부분을 영작하시오.515)

〈답〉

18. 위 글의 밑줄 친 부분을 영작하시오.516)

〈답〉

19. 위 글의 밑줄 친 부분을 영작하시오.517)

〈답〉

20. 위 지문을 참고하여 다음 요약문을 완성하시오.518)

〈요약〉 Dividing main topic with survival and _____the passage explains the _____of belonging for human _____

Many people make a mistake of only operating along the safe zones, and in the process they miss the opportunity to achieve greater things. They do so because of a fear of the unknown and a fear of treading the unknown paths of life. (1)_____
_____
_____. Being overcautious will mean that you will miss attaining the greatest levels of your potential. (2)_____
_____, (3)_____
_____
_____.

21. 위 글의 밑줄 친 부분을 영작하시오.519)

〈답〉

22. 위 글의 밑줄 친 부분을 영작하시오.520)

〈답〉

23. 위 글의 밑줄 친 부분을 영작하시오.521)

〈답〉

24. 위 지문을 참고하여 다음 요약문을 완성하시오.522)

〈요약〉 The passage _____readers to get out of the safe zones and be brave to take _____roads to attain the greatest levels of _____

2022년_고1_9월_인천광역시 교육청_학력평가_29번

The human brain, it turns out, has shrunk in mass by about 10 percent since it peaked in size 15,000-30,000 years ago. (1)_____
_____
_____. Today, we have effectively domesticated ourselves and many of the tasks of survival — from avoiding immediate death to building shelters to obtaining food — have been outsourced to the wider society. (2)_____
_____. (3)_____
_____
_____.

25. 위 글의 밑줄 친 부분을 영작하시오.523)

〈답〉

26. 위 글의 밑줄 친 부분을 영작하시오.524)

〈답〉

27. 위 글의 밑줄 친 부분을 영작하시오.525)

〈답〉

28. 위 지문을 참고하여 다음 요약문을 완성하시오.526)

〈요약〉 The passage on the _____size of human brain tries to find why it has, and _____that changed living _____ played a huge role.

2022년_고1_9월_인천광역시 교육청_학력평가_30번

It is widely believed that certain herbs somehow magically improve the work of certain organs, and "cure" specific diseases as a result. Such statements are unscientific and groundless. Sometimes herbs appear to work, since they tend to increase your blood circulation in an aggressive attempt by your body to eliminate them from your system. That can create a temporary feeling of a high, which makes it seem as if your health condition has improved. Also, herbs can have a placebo effect, just like any other method, thus helping you feel better. (1)_____
_____.
How can herbs have the intelligence needed to direct your body into getting healthier? That is impossible. (2)_____
_____. If you try to do that, you will see how impossible it seems. (3)_____
_____.

*placebo effect: 위약 효과

29. 위 글의 밑줄 친 부분을 영작하시오.527)

〈답〉

30. 위 글의 밑줄 친 부분을 영작하시오.528)

〈답〉

31. 위 글의 밑줄 친 부분을 영작하시오.529)

〈답〉

32. 위 지문을 참고하여 다음 요약문을 완성하시오.530)

〈요약〉 With the concept of bodily _____the passage tries to break _____misbelief that certain herbs can have _____effect on selective organs.

2022년_고1_9월_인천광역시 교육청_학력평가_31번

We worry that the robots are taking our jobs, but just as common a problem is that the robots are taking our judgment. In the large warehouses so common behind the scenes of today's economy, human 'pickers' hurry around (1)_____ _____. In their ears are headpieces: the voice of 'Jennifer', a piece of software, (2)___ _____ _____. Jennifer breaks down instructions into tiny chunks, to minimise error and maximise productivity — for example, rather than picking eighteen copies of a book off a shelf, the human worker would be politely instructed to pick five. Then another five. Then yet another five. Then another three. Working in such conditions reduces people to machines made of flesh. (3)_____, the Jennifer unit takes over the thought process and treats workers as an inexpensive source of some visual processing and a pair of opposable thumbs.

*dispatch: 발송하다 **chunk: 덩어리

33. 위 글의 밑줄 친 부분을 영작하시오.531)

〈답〉

34. 위 글의 밑줄 친 부분을 영작하시오.532)

〈답〉

35. 위 글의 밑줄 친 부분을 영작하시오.533)

〈답〉

36. 위 지문을 참고하여 다음 요약문을 완성하시오.534)

〈요약〉 By _____Jennifer, a piece of software, the passage _____that robots not only has taken our jobs but also our _____

2022년_고1_9월_인천광역시 교육청_학력평가_32번

The prevailing view among developmental scientists is that people are active contributors to their own development. (1)_____ _____, but they also play a role in influencing their development by interacting with, and changing, those contexts. Even infants influence the world around them and construct their own development through their interactions. Consider an infant who smiles at each adult he sees; he influences his world because adults are likely to smile, use "baby talk," and play with him in response. The infant brings adults into close contact, (2)_____ _____. (3)_____ _____ _____, individuals of all ages are "manufacturers of their own development."

37. 위 글의 밑줄 친 부분을 영작하시오.535)

〈답〉

38. 위 글의 밑줄 친 부분을 영작하시오.536)

〈답〉

39. 위 글의 밑줄 친 부분을 영작하시오.537)

〈답〉

40. 위 지문을 참고하여 다음 요약문을 완성하시오.538)

〈요약〉 Putting infant's _____on the center, the passage on developmental science provides an _____that individuals _____of ages can be an active contributor of development.

2022년_고1_9월_인천광역시 교육청_학력평가_33번

The demand for freshness can have hidden environmental costs. (1)_____ _____ in food marketing as part of a return to nature, the demand for year-round supplies of fresh produce such as soft fruit and exotic vegetables has led to the widespread use of hot houses in cold climates and increasing reliance on total quality control — management by temperature control, use of pesticides and computer/satellite-based logistics. The demand for freshness has also contributed to concerns about food wastage. Use of 'best before', 'sell by' and 'eat by' labels (2)_____. Campaigners have exposed the scandal of overproduction and waste. Tristram Stuart, one of the global band of anti-waste campaigners, argues that, (3)_____, over-ordering is standard practice across the retail sector to avoid the appearance of empty shelf space, leading to high volumes of waste when supply regularly exceeds demand.

* pesticide: 살충제 ** logistics: 물류, 유통

41. 위 글의 밑줄 친 부분을 영작하시오.539)

〈답〉

42. 위 글의 밑줄 친 부분을 영작하시오.540)

〈답〉

43. 위 글의 밑줄 친 부분을 영작하시오.541)

〈답〉

44. 위 지문을 참고하여 다음 요약문을 완성하시오.542)

〈요약〉 Alerting readers of the _____costs behind the demand for freshness, the passage introduces _____harms that is involved in the process of _____fresh foods.

2022년_고1_9월_인천광역시 교육청_학력평가_34번

In the studies of Colin Cherry at the Massachusetts Institute for Technology back in the 1950s, his participants listened to voices in one ear at a time and then through both ears in an effort to determine (1)_____ _____. One ear always (2)_____ _____ _____ _____. The trick was to see if you could totally focus on the main message and also hear someone talking in your other ear. Cleverly, Cherry (3)_____ _____ _____ __! In other words, people could not process two pieces of information at the same time.

45. 위 글의 밑줄 친 부분을 영작하시오.543)

〈답〉

46. 위 글의 밑줄 친 부분을 영작하시오.544)

〈답〉

47. 위 글의 밑줄 친 부분을 영작하시오.545)

〈답〉

48. 위 지문을 참고하여 다음 요약문을 완성하시오.546)

〈요약〉 Introducing an _____that has people hear two different messages _____the passage concludes that people cannot process two pieces of information _____

The fast-paced evolution of Information and Communication Technologies (ICTs) has radically transformed the dynamics and business models of the tourism and hospitality industry. This leads to new levels/forms of competitiveness among service providers and transforms the customer experience through new services. Creating unique experiences and providing convenient services to customers leads to satisfaction and, eventually, customer loyalty to the service provider or brand (i.e., hotels). In particular, (1)_____

_____. Indeed, (2)_____

_____

_____

_____.

* hospitality industry: 서비스업(호텔·식당업 등)

49. 위 글의 밑줄 친 부분을 영작하시오.547)

_____

〈답〉

_____

50. 위 글의 밑줄 친 부분을 영작하시오.548)

_____

〈답〉

_____

51. 위 지문을 참고하여 다음 요약문을 완성하시오.549)

_____

〈요약〉 _____what has happened with the evolution of ICTs, this passage links technological _____service provision and customer _____

With nearly a billion hungry people in the world, there is obviously no single cause. However, far and away the biggest cause is poverty. Seventy-nine percent of the world's hungry (1)_____

_____. How can this be? (2)___

_____

_____

_____. In the modern age you do not starve because you have no food, you starve because you have no money. So the problem really is that food is, in the grand scheme of things, too expensive and (3)_____

_. The answer will be in continuing the trend of lowering the cost of food.

* net exporter: 순 수출국 ** scheme: 체계, 조직

52. 위 글의 밑줄 친 부분을 영작하시오.550)

_____

〈답〉

_____

53. 위 글의 밑줄 친 부분을 영작하시오.551)

_____

〈답〉

_____

54. 위 글의 밑줄 친 부분을 영작하시오.552)

_____

〈답〉

_____

55. 위 지문을 참고하여 다음 요약문을 완성하시오.553)

_____

〈요약〉 The passage shortly _____the reason why people still _____despite _____food.

2022년_고1_9월_인천광역시 교육청_학력평가_37번

Most people have a perfect time of day (1)_____
_____, whether in the morning, evening, or afternoon. Some of us are night owls, some early birds, and others in between may feel most active during the afternoon hours. If you are able to organize your day and divide your work, (2)_____
_____. However, if the task you face demands creativity and novel ideas, it's best to tackle it at your "worst" time of day! So if you are an early bird, make sure to attack your creative task in the evening, and vice versa for night owls. When your mind and body are less alert than at your "peak" hours, (3)_____
_____. In other words, when your mental machinery is loose rather than standing at attention, the creativity flows.

*roam: (어슬렁어슬렁) 거닐다

56. 위 글의 밑줄 친 부분을 영작하시오.554)

〈답〉

57. 위 글의 밑줄 친 부분을 영작하시오.555)

〈답〉

58. 위 글의 밑줄 친 부분을 영작하시오.556)

〈답〉

59. 위 지문을 참고하여 다음 요약문을 완성하시오.557)

〈요약〉 The passage introduces _____insight that _____works best in the worst times of each individual.

2022년_고1_9월_인천광역시 교육청_학력평가_38번

Television is the number one leisure activity in the United States and Europe, consuming more than half of our free time. We generally think of television as a way to relax, tune out, and escape from our troubles for a bit each day. While this is true, (1)_____
_____ when we are feeling lonely or have a greater need for social connection. Television watching does satisfy these social needs to some extent, at least in the short run. Unfortunately, it is also likely to "crowd out" other activities that produce more sustainable social contributions to our social well-being. (2)_____
_____. In other words, (3)_____
_____.

*Friends: 프렌즈(미국의 한 방송국에서 방영된 시트콤)

60. 위 글의 밑줄 친 부분을 영작하시오.558)

〈답〉

61. 위 글의 밑줄 친 부분을 영작하시오.559)

〈답〉

62. 위 글의 밑줄 친 부분을 영작하시오.560)

〈답〉

63. 위 지문을 참고하여 다음 요약문을 완성하시오.561)

〈요약〉 This passage on the _____of television in terms of _____our social needs argues that television can _____ times for making real social networks.

2022년_고1_9월_인천광역시 교육청_학력평가_39번

(1)_____

_____

_____. In this way, our senses provide us with a qualitative indication of temperature. Our senses, however, are unreliable and often mislead us. For example, (2)_____

_____

_____. The two objects feel different (3)_____

_____. Your skin "measures" the rate of energy transfer by heat rather than the actual temperature. What we need is a reliable and reproducible method for measuring the relative hotness or coldness of objects rather than the rate of energy transfer. Scientists have developed a variety of thermometers for making such quantitative measurements.

*thermometer: 온도계

64. 위 글의 밑줄 친 부분을 영작하시오.562)

〈답〉

65. 위 글의 밑줄 친 부분을 영작하시오.563)

〈답〉

66. 위 글의 밑줄 친 부분을 영작하시오.564)

〈답〉

67. 위 지문을 참고하여 다음 요약문을 완성하시오.565)

〈요약〉 With an example situation of standing on two different _____with the same _____with each foot, the passage shows that our body cannot readily _____temperature.

2022년_고1_9월_인천광역시 교육청_학력평가_40번

My colleagues and I ran an experiment testing two different messages (1)_____

_____. One message emphasized the opportunity to do good: donating would benefit students, faculty, and staff. The other emphasized the opportunity to feel good: donors would enjoy the warm glow of giving. The two messages were equally effective: in both cases, 6.5 percent of the unwilling alumni ended up donating. Then we combined them, because two reasons are better than one. Except they weren't. When we put the two reasons together, the giving rate dropped below 3 percent. Each reason alone was (2)_____

_____. The audience was already skeptical. When we gave them different kinds of reasons to donate, (3)_____

_____

_____.

* alumni: 졸업생 ** skeptical: 회의적인

68. 위 글의 밑줄 친 부분을 영작하시오.566)

〈답〉

69. 위 글의 밑줄 친 부분을 영작하시오.567)

〈답〉

70. 위 글의 밑줄 친 부분을 영작하시오.568)

〈답〉

71. 위 지문을 참고하여 다음 요약문을 완성하시오.569)

〈요약〉 Through an experiment on making donation, the passage concludes that people _____themselves when they _____ the _____of persuasion.

2022년_고1_9월_인천광역시 교육청_학력평가_41~42번

In a society that rejects the consumption of insects there are some individuals who overcome this rejection, but most will continue with this attitude. It may be very difficult to convince an entire society that insects are totally suitable for consumption. However, there are examples (1)_____

_____

_____. Several examples in the past 120 years from European-American society are: considering lobster a luxury food instead of a food for servants and prisoners; considering sushi a safe and delicious food; and considering pizza not just a food for the rural poor of Sicily. In Latin American countries, where insects are already consumed, (2)_____

_____.

There are also examples of people who have had the habit of consuming them and abandoned that habit due to shame, and because they do not want to be categorized as poor or uncivilized. According to Esther Katz, an anthropologist, (3)_____

_____

_____

_____. And this could also help to revalue the consumption of insects by those people who already eat them.

72. 위 글의 밑줄 친 부분을 영작하시오.570)

<답>

73. 위 글의 밑줄 친 부분을 영작하시오.571)

<답>

74. 위 글의 밑줄 친 부분을 영작하시오.572)

<답>

75. 위 지문을 참고하여 다음 요약문을 완성하시오.573)

<요약> This passage on the social _____on the _____of certain food explores the _____psychology behind each attitude to certain foods.

고1 22년 9월 모의고사
변형문제 정답

어법 선택 (A)

18번
1) be held
2) requesting
3) clearly
4) listed
5) if
6) containing
7) as
8) carefully

19번
9) hadn't
10) hard I tapped
11) that
12) manage
13) have happened
14) picking
15) smoothly

20번
16) possible
17) word
18) something important
19) elaborate
20) While
21) equipped
22) distracted
23) what
24) it
25) using
26) used

21번
27) which
28) been abused
29) tried
30) to resolve
31) that
32) dissatisfied
33) are

22번
34) are
35) overstimulated
36) concentrating
37) distracted
38) support

23번
39) need
40) are

41) forming
42) to
43) want
44) survive
45) do

24번
46) because of
47) brave enough
48) travelled
49) are
50) derive
51) attaining
52) that

25번
53) that
54) that
55) ranked

26번
56) writing
57) to get
58) had
59) be
60) selling
61) although
62) published

27번
63) hosted on
64) If
65) starts
66) for
67) provided
68) canceled

28번
69) join
70) limited
71) team
72) provided

29번
73) shrunk
74) being
75) obtaining
76) that
77) wired

30번
78) appear
79) since
80) which
81) helping
82) that
83) has
84) come

85) impossible it seems
86) which
87) believe

31번
88) taking
89) dispatched
90) tells
91) controlling
92) instructed
93) reduces

32번
94) prevailing
95) is
96) in which
97) adult
98) because
99) smile
100) creating
101) interacting

33번
102) hidden
103) being used
104) has
105) contributed
106) has
107) exposed
108) campaigners
109) freshly
110) made
111) leading

34번
112) whether
113) talk
114) contained
115) included
116) see
117) it
118) for
119) spoken
120) was

35번
121) transformed
122) leads
123) received
124) is
125) represented
126) empowering
127) generates

36번
128) live
129) that
130) is
131) produced

132) pay
133) because
134) that
135) too
136) to buy

37번
137) are
138) active
139) that
140) demands
141) to attack
142) allowed
143) freely
144) flows

38번
145) consuming
146) While
147) motivated
148) satisfy
149) that
150) more
151) to spend
152) the
153) the

39번
154) an object feels
155) even though
156) are
157) different
158) because
159) does
160) What
161) developed

40번
162) meant
163) to make
164) donating
165) because
166) weren't
167) giving
168) effective
169) that
170) themselves
171) given
172) convinced

41~42번
173) It
174) that
175) in which
176) has
177) are
178) where
179) consumed
180) associates

181) due to
182) be categorized
183) poor
184) is
185) promoted
186) overcome
187) under which
188) educated

어휘 선택 (A)

20번

189) significant
190) eliminate
191) diverted
192) overlook
193) vital

21번

194) provides
195) intact
196) lay off
197) discontented

22번

198) confusion
199) worse
200) less
201) more
202) superfluous

23번

203) intense
204) advantageous
205) benefit
206) foster
207) multiple

24번

208) lose
209) less
210) able
211) derive
212) bold
213) discreet

26번

214) encouraged
215) rejections

29번

216) contracted
217) fierce

218) smaller
219) smaller
220) unintelligent

30번

221) enhance
222) illogical
223) boost
224) momentary
225) enhanced
226) implausible
227) more
228) hard

31번

229) usual
230) confines
231) cheap

32번

232) aggressive
233) modifying
234) likely

33번

235) novelty
236) extensive
237) increasing
238) permitted
239) revealed

34번

240) simultaneously
241) impossible

35번

242) evolution
243) results in
244) contentment

36번

245) plainly
246) more
247) because

37번

248) active
249) handle
250) arises
251) loose

38번

252) more
253) solitary
254) exclude
255) less

256) less

39번

257) incredible
258) equal
259) relative

40번

260) reluctant
261) doubtful

41~42번

262) refuses
263) proper
264) refuses
265) discarded
266) more

문장 넣기 (A)

267) ③
268) ⑤
269) ③
270) ②
271) ②
272) ⑤
273) ⑤
274) ③
275) ⑤
276) ④
277) ⑤
278) ④
279) ⑤
280) ④

순서 배열(A)

281) ① (A) - (C) - (B)
282) ⑤ (C) - (B) - (A)
283) ⑤ (C) - (B) - (A)
284) ② (B) - (A) - (C)
285) ② (B) - (A) - (C)
286) ② (B) - (A) - (C)
287) ④ (C) - (A) - (B)
288) ④ (C) - (A) - (B)
289) ① (A) - (C) - (B)
290) ③ (B) - (C) - (A)
291) ④ (C) - (A) - (B)
292) ① (A) - (C) - (B)
293) ① (A) - (C) - (B)
294) ① (A) - (C) - (B)
295) ① (A) - (C) - (B)
296) ③ (B) - (C) - (A)
297) ① (A) - (C) - (B)

298) ② (B) - (A) - (C)
299) ② (B) - (A) - (C)
300) ② (B) - (A) - (C)
301) ④ (C) - (A) - (B)
302) ④ (C) - (A) - (B)

연결어 선택(객관식)

22번

303) ④
23번

304) ④
30번

305) ④
34번

306) ③
36번

307) ①
37번

308) ②

어법 Lv_기본(객관식)

18번

309) ②
ⓒ what → that
ⓔ contained → containing

Dear Parents/Guardians, Class parties will be ⓐ <u>held</u> on the afternoon December 16th, 2022. Children may ⓑ <u>bring</u> in sweets, crisps, biscuits, cakes, and drinks. We are requesting ⓒ <u>that</u> children do not bring in home-cooked or prepared food. All food should arrive in a sealed packet with the ingredients clearly listed. Fruit and vegetables are welcomed ⓓ <u>if</u> they are pre-packed in a sealed packet from the shop. Please DO NOT send any food into school ⓔ <u>containing</u> nuts as we have many children with severe nut allergies. Please check the ingredients of all food your children bring ⓕ <u>carefully</u>. Thank you for your continued support and cooperation. Yours sincerely, Lisa Brown, Headteacher

19번

310) ③
ⓓ be managed → manage
ⓔ happen → have happened
ⓕ smooth → smoothly

It was two hours before the submission deadline and I still

ⓐ hadn't finished my news article. I sat at the desk, but suddenly, the typewriter didn't work. No matter how ⓑ hard I tapped the keys, the levers wouldn't move to strike the paper. I started to realize ⓒ that I would not be able to finish the article on time. Desperately, I rested the typewriter on my lap and started hitting each key with as much force as I could ⓓ be managed. Nothing happened. Thinking something might ⓔ have happened inside of it, I opened the cover, lifted up the keys, and found the problem — a paper clip. The keys had no room to move. After picking it out, I pressed and pulled some parts. The keys moved ⓕ smoothly again. I breathed deeply and smiled. Now I knew that I could finish my article on time.

20번

311) ④
ⓐ words → word
ⓑ isn't → doesn't
ⓓ equipping → equipped
ⓔ distracting → distracted

Experts on writing say, "Get rid of as many words as possible." Each ⓐ word must do something important. If it ⓑ doesn't, get rid of it. Well, this doesn't work for speaking. It takes more words to introduce, express, and adequately elaborate an idea in speech than it takes in writing. Why is this so? ⓒ While the reader can reread, the listener cannot rehear. Speakers do not come ⓓ equipped with a replay button. Because listeners are easily ⓔ distracted, they will miss many pieces of what a speaker says. If they miss the crucial sentence, they may never catch up. This makes it necessary for speakers to talk longer about their points, ⓕ using more words on them than would be used to express the same idea in writing.

21번

312) ③
ⓑ where → which
ⓓ abusing → abused
ⓕ is → are

Is the customer always right? When customers return a ⓐ broken product to a famous company, ⓑ which makes kitchen and bathroom fixtures, the company nearly always offers a replacement to maintain good customer relations. Still, "there are times you've got to ⓒ say 'no,'" explains the warranty expert of the company, such as when a product is undamaged or has been ⓓ abused. Entrepreneur Lauren Thorp, who owns an e-commerce company, says, "ⓔ While the customer is 'always' right, sometimes you just have to fire a customer." When Thorp has tried everything to resolve a complaint and realizes that the customer will be dissatisfied no matter what, she returns her attention to the rest of her customers, who she says ⓕ are "the reason for my success."

22번

313) ②
ⓒ concentrate → concentrating
ⓔ distracting → distracted

A recent study from Carnegie Mellon University in Pittsburgh, called "When Too Much of a Good Thing May Be Bad," indicates that classrooms with too much decoration are a source of distraction for young children and ⓐ directly affect their cognitive performance. ⓑ Being visually overstimulated, the children have a great deal of difficulty ⓒ concentrating and end up with worse academic results. On the other hand, ⓓ if there is not much decoration on the classroom walls, the children are less ⓔ distracted, spend more time on their activities, and learn more. So it's our job, in order to ⓕ support their attention, to find the right balance between excessive decoration and the complete absence of it.

23번

314) ②
ⓑ be shared → share
ⓕ what → who

For creatures like us, evolution smiled upon those with a strong need to belong. Survival and reproduction are the criteria of success by natural selection, and forming relationships with other people can be ⓐ useful for both survival and reproduction. Groups can ⓑ share resources, care for sick members, scare off predators, fight together against enemies, divide tasks so as to improve efficiency, and ⓒ contribute to survival in many other ways. In particular, if an individual and a group want the same resource, the group will generally prevail, so competition for resources would especially favor a need to belong. Belongingness will likewise ⓓ promote reproduction, such as by ⓔ bringing potential mates into contact with each other, and in particular by keeping parents together to care for their children, ⓕ who are much more likely to survive if they have more than one caregiver.

24번

315) ④
ⓐ are → do
ⓓ which → that
ⓔ what → that
ⓕ be flowed → flow

Many people make a mistake of only operating along the safe zones, and in the process they miss the opportunity to achieve greater things. They ⓐ do so because of a fear of the unknown and a fear of treading the unknown paths of life. Those that are ⓑ brave enough to take those roads less ⓒ travelled are able to get great returns and derive major satisfaction out of their courageous moves. Being overcautious will mean ⓓ that you will miss attaining the greatest levels of your potential. You must learn to take those chances ⓔ that many people around you will not take, because your success will ⓕ flow from those bold decisions that you will take along the way.

25번

316) ①

ⓑ was increased → increased

The graph above shows the share of the urban population by continent in 1950 and in 2020. For each ⓐ <u>continent</u>, the share of the urban population in 2020 was larger than that in 1950. From 1950 to 2020, the share of the urban population in Africa ⓑ <u>increased</u> from 14.3% to 43.5%. The share of the urban population in Asia ⓒ <u>was</u> the second lowest in 1950 but not in 2020. In 1950, the share of the urban population in Europe was larger than ⓓ <u>that</u> in Latin America and the Caribbean, whereas the reverse was true in 2020. Among the five continents, Northern America was ⓔ <u>ranked</u> in the first position for the share of the urban population in both 1950 and 2020.

26번

317) ④

ⓐ written → writing

ⓑ getting → to get

ⓔ sold → selling

ⓕ was resulted → resulted

Wilbur Smith was a South African novelist specialising in historical fiction. Smith wanted to become a journalist, ⓐ <u>writing</u> about social conditions in South Africa, but his father was never supportive of his writing and forced him ⓑ <u>to get</u> a real job. Smith studied further and became a tax accountant, but he finally turned back to his love of writing. He wrote his first novel, The Gods First Make Mad, and ⓒ <u>had</u> received 20 rejections by 1962. In 1964, Smith ⓓ <u>published</u> another novel, When the Lion Feeds, and it went on to be successful, ⓔ <u>selling</u> around the world. A famous actor and film producer bought the film rights for When the Lion Feeds, although no movie ⓕ <u>resulted</u>. By the time of his death in 2021 he had published 49 novels, selling more than 140 million copies worldwide.

29번

318) ⑤

ⓐ been shrunk → shrunk

ⓑ which → where

ⓓ obtain → obtaining

ⓔ what → that

ⓕ different → differently

The human brain, it turns out, has ⓐ <u>shrunk</u> in mass by about 10 percent since it peaked in size 15,000-30,000 years ago. One possible reason is that many thousands of years ago humans lived in a world of dangerous predators ⓑ <u>where</u> they had to have their wits about them at all times to avoid ⓒ <u>being killed</u>. Today, we have effectively domesticated ourselves and many of the tasks of survival

— from avoiding immediate death to building shelters to ⓓ <u>obtaining</u> food — have been outsourced to the wider society. We are smaller than our ancestors too, and it is a characteristic of domestic animals ⓔ <u>that</u> they are generally smaller than their wild cousins. None of this may mean we are dumber — brain size is not necessarily an indicator of human intelligence — but it may mean that our brains today are wired up ⓕ <u>differently</u>, and perhaps more efficiently, than those of our ancestors.

30번

319) ②

ⓒ that → which

ⓓ needing → needed

It is widely believed ⓐ <u>that</u> certain herbs somehow magically improve the work of certain organs, and "cure" specific diseases as a result. Such statements are unscientific and groundless. Sometimes herbs ⓑ <u>appear</u> to work, since they tend to increase your blood circulation in an aggressive attempt by your body to eliminate them from your system. That can create a temporary feeling of a high, ⓒ <u>which</u> makes it seem as if your health condition has improved. Also, herbs can have a placebo effect, just like any other method, thus helping you feel better. Whatever the case, it is your body that has the intelligence to regain health, and not the herbs. How can herbs have the intelligence ⓓ <u>needed</u> to direct your body into getting healthier? That is impossible. ⓔ <u>Try</u> to imagine how herbs might come into your body and intelligently fix your problems. If you try to do that, you will see how impossible it seems. Otherwise, it would mean that herbs are more intelligent than the human body, ⓕ <u>which</u> is truly hard to believe.

31번

320) ③

ⓒ dispatching → dispatched

ⓓ telling → tells

ⓕ treating → treats

We worry that the robots are ⓐ <u>taking</u> our jobs, but just as common a problem is that the robots are taking our judgment. In the large warehouses so common behind the scenes of today's economy, human 'pickers' hurry around grabbing products off shelves and ⓑ <u>moving</u> them to where they can be packed and ⓒ <u>dispatched</u>. In their ears are headpieces: the voice of 'Jennifer', a piece of software, ⓓ <u>tells</u> them where to go and what to do, controlling the smallest details of their movements. Jennifer breaks down instructions into tiny chunks, to minimise error and maximise productivity — for example, rather than picking eighteen copies of a book off a shelf, the human worker would be politely ⓔ <u>instructed</u> to pick five. Then another five. Then yet another five. Then another three. Working in such conditions reduces people to machines made of flesh. Rather than asking us to think or adapt, the Jennifer unit takes over the thought process and ⓕ <u>treats</u> workers

as an inexpensive source of some visual processing and a pair of opposable thumbs.

32번

321) ③
ⓐ are → is
ⓑ which → in which
ⓔ makes → making

The prevailing view among developmental scientists ⓐ is that people are active contributors to their own development. People are influenced by the physical and social contexts ⓑ in which they live, but they also play a role in influencing their development by interacting with, and changing, those contexts. Even infants ⓒ influence the world around them and construct their own development through their interactions. Consider an infant who smiles at each ⓓ adult he sees; he influences his world because adults are likely to smile, use "baby talk," and play with him in response. The infant brings adults into close contact, ⓔ making one-on-one interactions and creating opportunities for learning. By engaging the world around them, thinking, being curious, and ⓕ interacting with people, objects, and the world around them, individuals of all ages are "manufacturers of their own development."

33번

322) ②
ⓒ been contributed → contributed
ⓕ leads → leading

The demand for freshness can have hidden environmental costs. ⓐ While freshness is now being used as a term in food marketing as part of a return to nature, the demand for year-round supplies of fresh produce such as soft fruit and exotic vegetables has ⓑ led to the widespread use of hot houses in cold climates and increasing reliance on total quality control — management by temperature control, use of pesticides and computer/satellite-based logistics. The demand for freshness has also ⓒ contributed to concerns about food wastage. Use of 'best before', 'sell by' and 'eat by' labels has ⓓ legally allowed institutional waste. Campaigners have ⓔ exposed the scandal of overproduction and waste. Tristram Stuart, one of the global band of anti-waste campaigners, argues that, with freshly made sandwiches, over-ordering is standard practice across the retail sector to avoid the appearance of empty shelf space, ⓕ leading to high volumes of waste when supply regularly exceeds demand.

34번

323) ②
ⓔ of → for
ⓕ comprising → comprised

In the studies of Colin Cherry at the Massachusetts Institute for Technology back in the 1950s, his participants listened to voices in one ear at a time and then through both ears in an effort to determine   ⓐ whether we can listen to two people talk at the same time. One ear always ⓑ contained a message that the listener had to repeat back (called "shadowing") while   ⓒ the other ear included people speaking. The trick was to ⓓ see if you could totally focus on the main message and also hear someone talking in your other ear. Cleverly, Cherry found it was impossible ⓔ for his participants to know whether the message in the other ear was spoken by a man or woman, in English or another language, or was even ⓕ comprised of real words at all! In other words, people could not process two pieces of information at the same time.

35번

324) ③
ⓒ lead → leads
ⓓ receiving → received
ⓔ being → is

The fast-paced evolution of Information and Communication Technologies (ICTs) has ⓐ radically transformed the dynamics and business models of the tourism and hospitality industry. This leads to new levels/forms of competitiveness among service providers and ⓑ transforms the customer experience through new services. Creating unique experiences and providing convenient services to customers ⓒ leads to satisfaction and, eventually, customer loyalty to the service provider or brand (i.e., hotels). In particular, the most recent technological boost ⓓ received by the tourism sector   ⓔ is represented by mobile applications. Indeed,   ⓕ empowering tourists with mobile access to services such as hotel reservations, airline ticketing, and recommendations for local attractions generates strong interest and considerable profits.

36번

325) ③
ⓑ lives → live
ⓓ paying → pay
ⓕ so → too

With ⓐ nearly a billion hungry people in the world, there is obviously no single cause. However, far and away the biggest cause is poverty. Seventy-nine percent of the world's hungry ⓑ live in nations that are net exporters of food. How can this be? The reason people are hungry in those countries ⓒ is that the products produced there can be sold on the world market for more than the local citizens can afford to ⓓ pay for them. In the modern age you do not starve because you have no food, you starve ⓔ because you have no money. So the problem really is that food is, in the grand scheme of things, too expensive and many people are ⓕ <u>too</u> poor to buy it. The answer will be in continuing the trend of lowering the cost of food.

37번

326) ③
ⓑ making → make
ⓔ allowing → allowed
ⓕ is flowed → flows

Most people have a perfect time of day when they feel they are at their best, whether in the morning, evening, or afternoon. Some of us are night owls, some early birds, and ⓐ <u>others</u> in between may feel most active during the afternoon hours. If you are able to organize your day and divide your work, ⓑ <u>make</u> it a point to deal with tasks that demand attention at your best time of the day. However, if the task you face ⓒ <u>demands</u> creativity and novel ideas, it's best to tackle it at your "worst" time of day! So if you are an early bird, make sure ⓓ <u>to attack</u> your creative task in the evening, and vice versa for night owls. When your mind and body are less alert than at your "peak" hours, the muse of creativity awakens and is ⓔ <u>allowed</u> to roam more freely. In other words, when your mental machinery is loose rather than standing at attention, the creativity ⓕ <u>flows</u>.

38번

327) ④
ⓐ consumed → consuming
ⓒ motivating → motivated
ⓔ are produced → produce
ⓕ a → the

Television is the number one leisure activity in the United States and Europe, ⓐ <u>consuming</u> more than half of our free time. We generally think of television as a way to relax, tune out, and escape from our troubles for a bit each day. ⓑ <u>While</u> this is true, there is increasing evidence that we are more ⓒ <u>motivated</u> to tune in to our favorite shows and characters when we are feeling lonely or have a greater need for social connection. Television watching does ⓓ <u>satisfy</u> these social needs to some extent, at least in the short run. Unfortunately, it is also likely to "crowd out" other activities that ⓔ <u>produce</u> more sustainable social contributions to our social well-being. The more television we watch, the less likely we are to volunteer our time or to spend time with people in our social networks. In other words, the more time we make for Friends, ⓕ <u>the</u> less time we have for friends in real life.

39번

328) ④
ⓒ despite → even though
ⓓ is → does
ⓔ That → What
ⓕ been developed → developed

We often associate the concept of temperature with how hot or cold an object ⓐ <u>feels</u> when we touch it. In this way, our senses ⓑ <u>provide</u> us with a qualitative indication of temperature. Our senses, however, are unreliable and often mislead us. For example, if you stand in bare feet with one foot on carpet and the other on a tile floor, the tile feels colder than the carpet   ⓒ <u>even though</u> both are at the same temperature. The two objects feel different because tile transfers energy by heat at a higher rate than carpet ⓓ <u>does</u>. Your skin "measures" the rate of energy transfer by heat rather than the actual temperature. ⓔ <u>What</u> we need is a reliable and reproducible method for measuring the relative hotness or coldness of objects rather than the rate of energy transfer. Scientists have ⓕ <u>developed</u> a variety of thermometers for making such quantitative measurements.

40번

329) ④
ⓑ to donate → donating
ⓓ effectively → effective
ⓔ themselves → them
ⓕ convincing → convinced

My colleagues and I ran an experiment testing two different messages ⓐ <u>meant</u> to convince thousands of resistant alumni to make a donation. One message emphasized the opportunity to do good: donating would benefit students, faculty, and staff. The other emphasized the opportunity to feel good: donors would enjoy the warm glow of giving. The two messages were equally effective: in both cases, 6.5 percent of the unwilling alumni ended up ⓑ <u>donating</u>. Then we combined them, because two reasons are better than one. Except they ⓒ <u>weren't</u>. When we put the two reasons together, the giving rate dropped below 3 percent. Each reason alone was more than twice as ⓓ <u>effective</u> as the two combined. The audience was already skeptical. When we gave them different kinds of reasons to donate, we triggered their awareness that someone was trying to persuade ⓔ <u>them</u> — and they shielded themselves against it.

In the experiment mentioned above, when the two different reasons to donate were given simultaneously, the audience was less likely to be ⓕ <u>convinced</u> because they could recognize the intention to persuade them.

41-42번

330) ③
ⓑ which → in which
ⓓ associate → associates
ⓔ because → due to

In a society ⓐ <u>that</u> rejects the consumption of insects there are some individuals who overcome this rejection, but most will continue with this attitude. It may be very

difficult to convince an entire society that insects are totally suitable for consumption. However, there are examples ⓑ <u>in which</u> this reversal of attitudes about certain foods has happened to an entire society. Several examples in the past 120 years from European-American society are: considering lobster a luxury food instead of a food for servants and prisoners; considering sushi a safe and delicious food; and considering pizza not just a food for the rural poor of Sicily. In Latin American countries, where insects are already ⓒ <u>consumed</u>, a portion of the population hates their consumption and ⓓ <u>associates</u> it with poverty. There are also examples of people who have had the habit of consuming them and abandoned that habit ⓔ <u>due to</u> shame, and because they do not want to be categorized as poor or uncivilized. According to Esther Katz, an anthropologist, if the consumption of insects as a food luxury is to be promoted, there would be more chances that some individuals who do not present this habit overcome ideas ⓕ <u>under which</u> they were educated. And this could also help to revalue the consumption of insects by those people who already eat them.

어법 Lv_심화1(주관식)

18번
331)
① 틀린부분 : hold
　수정문장 : will be held on the afternoon December 16th, 2022
③ 틀린부분 : clear listing
　수정문장 : with the ingredients clear listed
⑤ 틀린부분 : due to
　수정문장 : as we have many children with severe nut allergies

19번
332)
① 틀린부분 : didn't
　수정문장 : I still hadn't finished my news article.
② 틀린부분 : I tapped hard
　수정문장 : No matter how hard I tapped the keys
④ 틀린부분 : due to
　수정문장 : as much force as I could manage

20번
333)
① 틀린부분 : words, important something
　수정문장 : Each word must do something important.
② 틀린부분 : elaborates
　수정문장 : and adequately elaborate an idea in speech
④ 틀린부분 : which
　수정문장 : they will miss many pieces of what a speaker says.

21번
334)
② 틀린부분 : has abused
　수정문장 : such as when a product is undamaged or has been abused
④ 틀린부분 : resolving
　수정문장 : When Thorp has tried everything to resolve a complaint and realizes
⑤ 틀린부분 : is
　수정문장 : who she says are "the reason for my success."

22번
335)
① 틀린부분 : being
　수정문장 : with too much decoration are a source of distraction for young children
③ 틀린부분 : concentrated
　수정문장 : the children have a great deal of difficulty concentrating and end up with worse academic results
⑤ 틀린부분 : supporting
　수정문장 : in order to support their attention

23번
336)
① 틀린부분 : needed
　수정문장 : with a strong need to belong
② 틀린부분 : formed
　수정문장 : and forming relationships with other people can be useful for both survival and reproduction
⑤ 틀린부분 : surviving
　수정문장 : who are much more likely to survive if they have more than one caregiver.

24번
337)
① 틀린부분 : are
　수정문장 : They do so
③ 틀린부분 : travelling
　수정문장 : to take those roads less travelled
⑤ 틀린부분 : to attain
　수정문장 : you will miss attaining the greatest levels of your potentia

25번
338)
② 틀린부분 : increasing
　수정문장 : the share of the urban population in Africa increased from 14.3% to 43.5%
④ 틀린부분 : it
　수정문장 : larger than that in Latin America
⑤ 틀린부분 : ranking
　수정문장 : Northern America was ranked in the first position for the share of the urban population in

both 1950 and 2020

26번
339)
① 틀린부분 : wrote
　수정문장 : writing about social conditions in South Africa
③ 틀린부분 : was
　수정문장 : The Gods First Make Mad, and had received 20 rejections by 1962
④ 틀린부분 : being
　수정문장 : it went on to be successful, selling around the world

27번
340)
① 틀린부분 : hosting
　수정문장 : Enjoy yoga hosted on the park lawn
③ 틀린부분 : will start
　수정문장 : At least TWO hours before each class starts
⑤ 틀린부분 : cancel
　수정문장 : The class will be canceled

28번
341)
③ 틀린부분 : join with
　수정문장 : Participants must enter in teams of four and can only join one team
④ 틀린부분 : teams
　수정문장 : Submission is limited to one proposal per team
⑤ 틀린부분 : providing
　수정문장 : Participants must use the proposal form provided on the website

29번
342)
① 틀린부분 : was peaked
　수정문장 : since it peaked in size 15,000-30,000 years ago
② 틀린부분 : what, to be
　수정문장 : where they had to have their wits about them at all times to avoid being killed
④ 틀린부분 : which
　수정문장 : that they are generally smaller than their wild cousins

30번
343)
① 틀린부분 : are appeared
　수정문장 : Sometimes herbs appear to work
④ 틀린부분 : be come, fixing
　수정문장 : Try to imagine how herbs might come into your body and intelligently fix your problems
⑤ 틀린부분 : it seems impossible
　수정문장 : you will see how impossible it seems

31번
344)
② 틀린부분 : dispatch
　수정문장 : moving them to where they can be packed and dispatched
③ 틀린부분 : controls
　수정문장 : controlling the smallest details of their movements
④ 틀린부분 : instructing
　수정문장 : the human worker would be politely instructed to pick five

32번
345)
② 틀린부분 : which
　수정문장 : by the physical and social contexts in which they live
③ 틀린부분 : adults
　수정문장 : Consider an infant who smiles at each adult he sees
⑤ 틀린부분 : creates
　수정문장 : making one-on-one interactions and creating opportunities for learning

33번
346)
② 틀린부분 : using
　수정문장 : freshness is now being used as a term in food marketing as part of a return to nature
④ 틀린부분 : have been exposed
　수정문장 : Campaigners have exposed the scandal of overproduction and waste
⑤ 틀린부분 : leads
　수정문장 : leading to high volumes of waste when supply regularly exceeds demand

34번
347)
① 틀린부분 : what
　수정문장 : whether we can listen to two people talk at the same time
③ 틀린부분 : including
　수정문장 : while the other ear included people speaking
④ 틀린부분 : them, of
　수정문장 : Cherry found it was impossible for his participants

35번
348)
② 틀린부분 : leading
　수정문장 : leads to satisfaction and, eventually, customer loyalty to the service provider or brand

④ 틀린부분 : being empowering

수정문장 : empowering tourists with mobile access to services

⑤ 틀린부분 : generating

수정문장 : recommendations for local attractions generates strong interest and considerable profits

36번
349)

② 틀린부분 : produce

수정문장 : that the products produced there can be sold on the world market

④ 틀린부분 : which

수정문장 : So the problem really is that food is

⑤ 틀린부분 : so, buying

수정문장 : too expensive and many people are too poor to buy it

37번
350)

① 틀린부분 : being

수정문장 : when they feel they are at their best

③ 틀린부분 : demanding

수정문장 : if the task you face demands creativity and novel ideas

⑤ 틀린부분 : is flowed

수정문장 : the creativity flows

38번
351)

① 틀린부분 : consumes

수정문장 : consuming more than half of our free time

③ 틀린부분 : satisfying

수정문장 : Television watching does satisfy these social needs to some extent,

⑤ 틀린부분: spending

수정문장 : to spend time with people in our social networks

39번
352)

① 틀린부분 : feels an object

수정문장 : with how hot or cold an object feels

③ 틀린부분 : is

수정문장 : because tile transfers energy by heat at a higher rate than carpet does

⑤ 틀린부분 : have been developed

수정문장 : Scientists have developed a variety of thermometers for making such quantitative measurements

40번
353)

① 틀린부분 : meaning, making

수정문장 : meant to convince thousands of resistant alumni to make a donation

② 틀린부분 : donated

수정문장 : 6.5 percent of the unwilling alumni ended up donating

④ 틀린부분 : effectively

수정문장 : Each reason alone was more than twice as effective as the two combined

41~42번
354)

③ 틀린부분 : being

수정문장 : Several examples in the past 120 years from European-American society are

④ 틀린부분 : hate, associate

수정문장 : a portion of the population hates their consumption and associates it with poverty

⑤ 틀린부분 : overcoming, which

수정문장 : some individuals who do not present this habit overcome ideas under which they were educated

어법 Lv_심화2(주관식)

18번
355)

Dear Parents/Guardians, Class parties will ①hold→be held on the afternoon December 16th, 2022. Children may bring in sweets, crisps, biscuits, cakes, and drinks. We are ②requested→requesting that children do not bring in home-cooked or prepared food. All food should arrive in a sealed packet with the ingredients ③clear→clearly listed. Fruit and vegetables are welcomed if they are pre-packed in a sealed packet from the shop. Please DO NOT send any food into school ④contained→containing nuts due to we have many children with severe nut allergies. Please check the ingredients of all food your children bring ⑤careful→carefully. Thank you for your continued support and cooperation. Yours sincerely, Lisa Brown, Headteacher

19번
356)

It was two hours before the submission deadline and I still ①haven't→hadn't finished my news article. I sat at the desk, but suddenly, the typewriter didn't work. No matter how ②I tapped hard→hard I tapped the keys, the levers wouldn't move to strike the paper. I started to realize ③which→that I would not be able to finish the article on time.

Desperately, I rested the typewriter on my lap and started hitting each key with as much force as I could ④be managed→manage. Nothing happened. Thinking something might have happened inside of it, I opened the cover, lifted up the keys, and found the problem — a paper clip. The keys had no room to move. After ⑤picked→picking it out, I pressed and pulled some parts. The keys moved smoothly again. I breathed deeply and smiled. Now I knew that I could finish my article on time.

20번
357)

Experts on writing say, "Get rid of as many words as ①possibly→possible." Each ②words→word must do something important. If it doesn't, get rid of it. Well, this doesn't work for speaking. It takes more words to introduce, express, and adequately ③ elaborates→elaborate an idea in speech than it takes in writing. Why is this so? While the reader can reread, the listener cannot rehear. Speakers do not come ④equip→equipped with a replay button. Because listeners are easily distracted, they will miss many pieces of ⑤that→what a speaker says. If they miss the crucial sentence, they may never catch up. This makes it necessary for speakers to talk longer about their points, using more words on them than would be used to express the same idea in writing.

21번
358)

Is the customer always right? When customers return a broken product to a famous company, ① what→which makes kitchen and bathroom fixtures, the company nearly always offers a replacement to maintain good customer relations. Still, "there are times you've got to say 'no,'" explains the warranty expert of the company, such as when a product is undamaged or has ②abused→been abused. Entrepreneur Lauren Thorp, who owns an e-commerce company, says, "While the customer is 'always' right, sometimes you just have to fire a customer." When Thorp has ③been tried→tried everything to resolve a complaint and realizes that the customer will be ④dissatisfying→dissatisfied no matter what, she returns her attention to the rest of her customers, who she says ⑤is→are "the reason for my success."

22번
359)

A recent study from Carnegie Mellon University in Pittsburgh, called "When Too Much of a Good Thing May Be Bad," indicates that classrooms with too much decoration ①is→are a source of distraction for young children and directly affect their cognitive performance. Being visually ② overstimulating→overstimulated, the children have a great deal of difficulty ③concentrate→concentrating and end up with worse academic results. On the other hand, if there is not much decoration on the classroom walls, the children are less ④distracting→distracted, spend more time on their activities, and learn more. So it's our job, in order to ⑤supporting →support their attention, to find the right balance between excessive decoration and the complete absence of it.

23번
360)

For creatures like us, evolution smiled upon those with a strong ①needed→need to belong. Survival and reproduction ②being→are the criteria of success by natural selection, and ③formed→forming relationships with other people can be useful for both survival and reproduction. Groups can share resources, care for sick members, scare off predators, fight together against enemies, divide tasks so as ④for improving→to improving efficiency, and contribute to survival in many other ways. In particular, if an individual and a group ⑤wants→ want the same resource, the group will generally prevail, so competition for resources would especially favor a need to belong. Belongingness will likewise promote reproduction, such as by bringing potential mates into contact with each other, and in particular by keeping parents together to care for their children, who are much more likely to survive if they have more than one caregiver.

24번
361)

Many people make a mistake of only operating along the safe zones, and in the process they miss the opportunity to achieve greater things. They ①are →do so ②because→because of a fear of the unknown and a fear of treading the unknown paths of life. Those that are ③enough brave→brave enough to take those roads less ④travelling→ travelled are able to get great returns and derive major satisfaction out of their courageous moves. Being overcautious will mean that you will miss attaining the greatest levels of your potential. You must learn to take those chances ⑤what→that

many people around you will not take, because your success will flow from those bold decisions that you will take along the way.

25번
362)

The graph above ①showing→shows the share of the urban population by continent in 1950 and in 2020. For each continent, the share of the urban population in 2020 was larger than ②it→that in 1950. From 1950 to 2020, the share of the urban population in Africa ③increasing→increased from 14.3% to 43.5%. The share of the urban population in Asia was the second lowest in 1950 but not in 2020. In 1950, the share of the urban population in Europe was larger than ④those→that in Latin America and the Caribbean, whereas the reverse was true in 2020. Among the five continents, Northern America was ⑤ranking→ranked in the first position for the share of the urban population in both 1950 and 2020.

26번
363)

Wilbur Smith was a South African novelist specialising in historical fiction. Smith wanted to become a journalist, ①written→writing about social conditions in South Africa, but his father was never supportive of his writing and forced him ②getting→to get a real job. Smith studied further and became a tax accountant, but he finally turned back to his love of writing. He wrote his first novel, The Gods First Make Mad, and ③was→had received 20 rejections by 1962. In 1964, Smith published another novel, When the Lion Feeds, and it went on to ④being→be successful, selling around the world. A famous actor and film producer bought the film rights for When the Lion Feeds, although no movie resulted. By the time of his death in 2021 he had ⑤been published→published 49 novels, selling more than 140 million copies worldwide.

27번
364)

2022 Springfield Park Yoga Class
The popular yoga class in Springfield Park returns! Enjoy yoga ①hosting→hosted on the park lawn. ② Unless→If you can't make it to the park, join us online on our social media platforms!
◆When: Saturdays, 2 p.m. to 3 p.m., September
◆Registration: At least TWO hours before each class ③will start→starts, sign up here.

◆Notes
•For online classes: find a quiet space with enough room ④of→for you to stretch out.
•For classes in the park: mats are not ⑤providing→ provided, so bring your own!
※The class will be canceled if the weather is unfavorable. For more information, click here.

28번
365)

Kenner High School's Water Challenge
Kenner High School's Water Challenge is a new contest ①proposed→to propose measures against water pollution. Please share your ideas for dealing with water pollution!
Submission
How: Submit your proposal by email to admin@khswater.edu.
When: September 5, 2022 to September 23, 2022
Details
Participants must enter in teams of four and can only ②join with→join one team.
Submission is ③limiting→limited to one proposal per ④teams→team.
Participants must use the proposal form ⑤provide→ provided on the website.
Prizes
1st: $50 gift certificate
2nd: $30 gift certificate
3rd: $10 gift certificate
Please visit www.khswater.edu to learn more about the challenge.

29번
366)

The human brain, it turns out, has ①been shrunk→ shrunk in mass by about 10 percent since it peaked in size 15,000-30,000 years ago. One possible reason is that many thousands of years ago humans lived in a world of dangerous predators ②what→ where they had to have their wits about them at all times to avoid ③to be→being killed. Today, we have effectively domesticated ourselves and many of the tasks of survival — from avoiding immediate death to building shelters to obtaining food — ④has→ have been outsourced to the wider society. We are smaller than our ancestors too, and it is a characteristic of domestic animals ⑤which→that they are generally smaller than their wild cousins. None of this may mean we are dumber — brain size is not necessarily an indicator of human intelligence — but it may mean that our brains today are wired up

differently, and perhaps more efficiently, than those of our ancestors.

30번
367)

It is widely believed that certain herbs somehow magically improve the work of certain organs, and "cure" specific diseases as a result. Such statements are unscientific and groundless. Sometimes herbs ① are appeared→appear to work, since they tend to increase your blood circulation in an aggressive attempt by your body to eliminate them from your system. That can create a temporary feeling of a high, ②that→which makes it seem as if your health condition has improved. Also, herbs can have a placebo effect, just like any other method, thus ③ helped→helping you feel better. Whatever the case, it is your body ④which→that has the intelligence to regain health, and not the herbs. How can herbs have the intelligence needed to direct your body into getting healthier? That is impossible. Try to imagine how herbs might ⑤be come→come into your body and intelligently fix your problems. If you try to do that, you will see how impossible it seems. Otherwise, it would mean that herbs are more intelligent than the human body, which is truly hard to believe.

31번
368)

We worry that the robots are taking our jobs, but just as common a problem is that the robots are taking our judgment. In the large warehouses so common behind the scenes of today's economy, human 'pickers' hurry around grabbing products off shelves and moving them to where they can be packed and ①dispatch→dispatched. In their ears are headpieces: the voice of 'Jennifer', a piece of software, ②tell→tells them where to go and what to do, ③controls→controlling the smallest details of their movements. Jennifer breaks down instructions into tiny chunks, to minimise error and maximise productivity — for example, rather than picking eighteen copies of a book off a shelf, the human worker would be politely instructed to pick five. Then another five. Then yet another five. Then another three. Working in such conditions ④reduce →reduces people to machines made of flesh. Rather than asking us to think or adapt, the Jennifer unit takes over the thought process and ⑤treating→ treats workers as an inexpensive source of some visual processing and a pair of opposable thumbs.

32번
369)

The ①prevailed→prevailing view among developmental scientists ②are→is that people are active contributors to their own development. People are influenced by the physical and social contexts ③ which→in which they live, but they also play a role in influencing their development by interacting with, and changing, those contexts. Even infants influence the world around them and construct their own development through their interactions. Consider an infant who smiles at each adult he sees; he influences his world because adults are likely to ④ smiling→smile, use "baby talk," and play with him in response. The infant brings adults into close contact, making one-on-one interactions and creating opportunities for learning. By engaging the world around them, thinking, being curious, and ⑤interact →interacting with people, objects, and the world around them, individuals of all ages are "manufacturers of their own development."

33번

The demand for freshness can have ①hiding→ hidden environmental costs. While freshness is now being used as a term in food marketing as part of a return to nature, the demand for year-round supplies of fresh produce such as soft fruit and exotic vegetables ②have→has led to the widespread use of hot houses in cold climates and increasing reliance on total quality control — management by temperature control, use of pesticides and computer/satellite-based logistics. The demand for freshness has also contributed to concerns about food wastage. Use of 'best before', 'sell by' and 'eat by' labels has legally allowed institutional waste. Campaigners have ③been exposed→exposed the scandal of overproduction and waste. Tristram Stuart, one of the global band of anti-waste ④ campaigner→campaigners, argues that, with freshly made sandwiches, over-ordering is standard practice across the retail sector to avoid the appearance of empty shelf space, ⑤led→leading to high volumes of waste when supply regularly exceeds demand.

34번
371)

In the studies of Colin Cherry at the Massachusetts Institute for Technology back in the 1950s, his participants listened to voices in one ear at a time and then through both ears in an effort to

determine ①what→whether we can listen to two people ②talked→talk at the same time. One ear always contained a message that the listener had to repeat back (called "shadowing") while the other ear included people speaking. The trick was to ③seeing →see if you could totally focus on the main message and also hear someone talking in your other ear. Cleverly, Cherry found it was impossible ④of→for his participants to know whether the message in the other ear was ⑤speaking→spoken by a man or woman, in English or another language, or was even comprised of real words at all! In other words, people could not process two pieces of information at the same time.

35번
372)

The fast-paced evolution of Information and Communication Technologies (ICTs) has radically ① been transformed→transformed the dynamics and business models of the tourism and hospitality industry. This leads to new levels/forms of competitiveness among service providers and transforms the customer experience through new services. Creating unique experiences and providing convenient services to customers ②lead→leads to satisfaction and, eventually, customer loyalty to the service provider or brand (i.e., hotels). In particular, the most recent technological boost ③receiving→ received by the tourism sector ④are→is represented by mobile applications. Indeed, empowering tourists with mobile access to services such as hotel reservations, airline ticketing, and recommendations for local attractions ⑤generated→generates strong interest and considerable profits.

36번
373)

With nearly a billion hungry people in the world, there is obviously no single cause. However, far and away the biggest cause is poverty. Seventy-nine percent of the world's hungry ①lives→live in nations ②what→that are net exporters of food. How can this be? The reason people are hungry in those countries is that the products produced there can be sold on the world market for more than the local citizens can afford to ③paying→pay for them. In the modern age you do not starve because you have no food, you starve because you have no money. So the problem really is ④which→that food is, in the grand scheme of things, too expensive and many people are too poor ⑤buying→to buy it.

The answer will be in continuing the trend of lowering the cost of food.

37번
374)

Most people have a perfect time of day when they feel they are at their best, whether in the morning, evening, or afternoon. Some of us are night owls, some early birds, and others in between may feel most ①actively→active during the afternoon hours. If you are able to organize your day and divide your work, make it a point to deal with tasks ②what→ that demand attention at your best time of the day. However, if the task you face ③demand→demands creativity and novel ideas, it's best to tackle it at your "worst" time of day! So if you are an early bird, make sure to attack your creative task in the evening, and vice versa for night owls. When your mind and body are less alert than at your "peak" hours, the muse of creativity awakens and is allowed to roam more ④free→freely. In other words, when your mental machinery is loose rather than standing at attention, the creativity ⑤is flowed →flows.

38번
375)

Television is the number one leisure activity in the United States and Europe, ①consumed→consuming more than half of our free time. We generally think of television as a way to relax, tune out, and escape from our troubles for a bit each day. ② During→While this is true, there is increasing evidence that we are more motivated to tune in to our favorite shows and characters when we are feeling lonely or have a greater need for social connection. Television watching does ③satisfies→ satisfy these social needs to some extent, at least in the short run. Unfortunately, it is also likely to "crowd out" other activities ④in which→that produce more sustainable social contributions to our social well-being. The ⑤most→more television we watch, the less likely we are to volunteer our time or to spend time with people in our social networks. In other words, the more time we make for Friends, the less time we have for friends in real life.

39번
376)

We often associate the concept of temperature with how hot or cold ①feels an object→an object feels when we touch it. In this way, our senses provide

us with a qualitative indication of temperature. Our senses, however, are unreliable and often mislead us. For example, if you stand in bare feet with one foot on carpet and the other on a tile floor, the tile feels colder than the carpet ②despite→even though both are at the same temperature. The two objects feel ③differently→different because tile transfers energy by heat at a higher rate than carpet ④is→ does. Your skin "measures" the rate of energy transfer by heat rather than the actual temperature. What we need is a reliable and reproducible method for measuring the relative hotness or coldness of objects rather than the rate of energy transfer. Scientists have ⑤been developed→ developed a variety of thermometers for making such quantitative measurements.

40번
377)

My colleagues and I ran an experiment testing two different messages meant to convince thousands of resistant alumni ①making→to make a donation. One message emphasized the opportunity to do good: donating would benefit students, faculty, and staff. The other emphasized the opportunity to feel good: donors would enjoy the warm glow of giving. The two messages were equally effective: in both cases, 6.5 percent of the unwilling alumni ended up ② donated→donating. Then we combined them, ③ because→because of two reasons are better than one. Except they ④didn't→weren't. When we put the two reasons together, the giving rate dropped below 3 percent. Each reason alone was more than twice as effective as the two combined. The audience was already skeptical. When we gave them different kinds of reasons to donate, we triggered their awareness ⑤which→that someone was trying to persuade them — and they shielded themselves against it.

In the experiment mentioned above, when the two different reasons to donate were given simultaneously, the audience was less likely to be convinced because they could recognize the intention to persuade them.

41~42번
378)

In a society that rejects the consumption of insects there are some individuals who overcome this rejection, but most will continue with this attitude. ①That→It may be very difficult to convince an entire society ②what→that insects are totally suitable for consumption. However, there are examples in which this reversal of attitudes about certain foods ③have →has happened to an entire society. Several examples in the past 120 years from European-American society are: considering lobster a luxury food instead of a food for servants and prisoners; considering sushi a safe and delicious food; and considering pizza not just a food for the rural poor of Sicily. In Latin American countries, ④ which→where insects are already consumed, a portion of the population hates their consumption and associates it with poverty. There are also examples of people who have had the habit of consuming them and abandoned that habit due to shame, and because they do not want to ⑤ categorize→be categorized as poor or uncivilized. According to Esther Katz, an anthropologist, if the consumption of insects as a food luxury is to be promoted, there would be more chances that some individuals who do not present this habit overcome ideas under which they were educated. And this could also help to revalue the consumption of insects by those people who already eat them.

서술형 Lv_기본

379) All food should arrive in a sealed packet with the ingredients clearly listed.
380) Precautions for Attending Class Parties
381) the ingredients of all food your children bring carefully.

382) No matter how hard I tapped the keys, the levers wouldn't move to strike the paper.
383) Why Is The Typewriter Not Working?
384) Thinking something might have happened inside of it

385) t takes more words to introduce, express, and adequately elaborate an idea in speech than it takes in writing.
386) More Words Make a Better Speech
387) This makes it necessary for speakers to talk longer about their points.
388) Still, "there are times you've got to say 'no,'" explains the warranty expert of the company, such as when a product is undamaged or has

been abused.

389) Is The Customer Always Right?

390) attention to the rest of her customers, who she says are "the reason for my success."

391) Being visually overstimulated, the children have a great deal of difficulty concentrating and end up with worse academic results.

392) Classroom Decoration: Poison or Medicine?

393) to find the right balance between excessive decoration and the complete absence of it.

394) In particular, if an individual and a group want the same resource, the group will generally prevail, so competition for resources would especially favor a need to belong.

395) The Evolutionary Help of Belonging

396) who are much more likely to survive if they have more than one caregiver.

397) You must learn to take those chances that many people around you will not take

398) What You Need to Take for Success

399) those bold decisions that you will take along the way.

400) We are smaller than our ancestors too, and it is a characteristic of domestic animals that they are generally smaller than their wild cousins.

401) Changes in Brain Size Due to The Environment

402) but it may mean that our brains today are wired up differently

403) Whatever the case, it is your body that has the intelligence to regain health, and not the herbs.

404) Herb: It Is Not a Panacea

405) how herbs might come into your body and intelligently fix your problems.

406) In their ears are headpieces: the voice of 'Jennifer', a piece of software, tells them where to go and what to do, controlling the smallest details of their movements.

407) What Robots Take from Humans

408) Rather than asking us to think or adapt

409) The infant brings adults into close contact, making one-on-one interactions and creating opportunities for learning.

410) What Contributes to Our Development?

411) By engaging the world around them, thinking, being curious, and interacting with people, objects, and the world around them

412) While freshness is now being used as a term in food marketing as part of a return to nature

413) The Price Hidden in Freshness

414) with freshly made sandwiches

415) One ear always contained a message that the listener had to repeat back (called "shadowing") while the other ear included people speaking.

416) What Is Interesting about People's Information Processing

417) whether we can listen to two people talk at the same time

418) In particular, the most recent technological boost received by the tourism sector is represented by mobile applications.

419) Evolution and Butterfly Effect of Technology

420) empowering tourists with mobile access to services such as hotel reservations, airline ticketing, and recommendations for local attractions generates strong interest and considerable profits.

421) Seventy-nine percent of the world's hungry live in nations that are net exporters of food.

422) Poverty: Food Shortages Are Not The Cause

423) many people are too poor to buy it.

424) Most people have a perfect time of day when they feel they are at their best, whether in the morning, evening, or afternoon.

425) Task To Do during The Worst Time

426) make it a point to deal with tasks that demand attention at your best time of the day

427) The more television we watch, the less likely we are to volunteer our time or to spend time with people in our social networks.

428) The Trap of Watching Television

429) the more time we make for Friends, the less time we have for friends in real life.

430) We often associate the concept of temperature with how hot or cold an object feels when we touch it.

431) The Reason Why We Feel The Temperature Wrong

432) because tile transfers energy by heat at a higher rate than carpet does

433) Each reason alone was more than twice as effective as the two combined.

434) A Point of Caution When Convincing A Person

435) we triggered their awareness that someone was

trying to persuade them — and they shielded themselves against it

436) However, there are examples in which this reversal of attitudes about certain foods has happened to an entire society.
437) A Reversal of One's Attitude toward A Particular Food
438) a portion of the population hates their consumption and associates it with poverty

서술형 Lv_심화1

439) All food should arrive in a sealed packet with the ingredients clearly listed.
440) It is an article that delivers information about the food brought to the class parties.
441) Please check the ingredients of all food your children bring carefully.

442) No matter how hard I tapped the keys, the levers wouldn't move to strike the paper.
443) The typewriter broke down for a while because of the paper clip.
444) Desperately, I rested the typewriter on my lap and started hitting each key with as much force as I could manage.

445) This makes it necessary for speakers to talk longer about their points.
446) Unlike writing, more words should be used in speaking.
447) It takes more words to introduce, express, and adequately elaborate an idea in speech than it takes in writing.

448) such as when a product is undamaged or has been abused.
449) Sometimes there should be times when the company reject the customer's request.
450) She returns her attention to the rest of her customers, who she says are "the reason for my success."

451) the children are less distracted, spend more time on their activities, and learn more.
452) Classroom decorations that affect children's learning should be appropriately utilized.
453) Being visually overstimulated, the children have a great deal of difficulty concentrating and end up

with worse academic results.

454) so competition for resources would especially favor a need to belong.
455) Belonging is useful for human evolution.
456) divide tasks so as to improve efficiency, and contribute to survival in many other ways.

457) You must learn to take those chances that many people around you will not take
458) Success comes from brave decisions in the course of life.
459) Your success will flow from those bold decisions that you will take along the way

460) it is a characteristic of domestic animals that they are generally smaller than their wild cousins
461) Our brains are smaller than in the past.
462) but it may mean that our brains today are wired up differently

463) Whatever the case, it is your body that has the intelligence to regain health, and not the herbs.
464) Herbs don't make us healthier.
465) how herbs might come into your body and intelligently fix your problems.

466) tells them where to go and what to do, controlling the smallest details of their movements.
467) Robots are taking away human judgment.
468) Rather than asking us to think or adapt,

469) People are influenced by the physical and social contexts in which they live,
470) People actively contribute their own development.
471) By engaging the world around them, thinking, being curious, and interacting with people, objects, and the world around them,

472) has legally allowed institutional waste.
473) The demand for freshness has a variety of environmental costs.
474) with freshly made sandwiches

475) to determine whether we can listen to two people talk at the same time.
476) People cannot process two pieces of information at the same time.
477) found it was impossible for his participants to know whether the message in the other ear was spoken by a man or woman, in English or another language, or was even comprised of real

words at all!

478) empowering tourists with mobile access to services such as hotel reservations, airline ticketing, and recommendations for local attractions generates strong interest and considerable profits.

479) Information and communication technologies has dynamically changed the tourism and hospitality industries.

480) the most recent technological boost received by the tourism sector is represented by mobile applications.

481) many people are too poor to buy it.

482) People go hungry because they don't have money other than food.

483) live in nations that are net exporters of food.

484) when they feel they are at their best

485) It is good to perform tasks that require creativity and new ideas at the worst time of an individual.

486) the muse of creativity awakens and is allowed to roam more freely.

487) The more television we watch, the less likely we are to volunteer our time or to spend time with people in our social networks.

488) Watching television is easy to limit activities for our social well-being.

489) the more time we make for Friends, the less time we have for friends in real life.

490) We often associate the concept of temperature with how hot or cold an object feels when we touch it.

491) Our skin measures the rate of energy transfer by heat, not actual temperature.

492) because tile transfers energy by heat at a higher rate than carpet does.

493) Each reason alone was was more than twice as effective as the two combined.

494) People find it harder to be convinced when they notice the intentions to persuade them.

495) we triggered their awareness that someone was trying to persuade them — and they shielded themselves against it.

496) However, there are examples in which this reversal of attitudes about certain foods has happened to an entire society.

497) It is difficult to reverse the attitude toward certain foods, but it also occurs throughout society and has many effects.

498) a portion of the population hates their consumption and associates it with poverty.

서술형 Lv_심화2

499) All food should arrive in a sealed packet with the ingredients clearly listed

500) Please check the ingredients of all food your children bring carefully

501) Please check the ingredients of all food your children bring carefully

502) The letter outlines several **rules** and requests on the food that children **may** bring to the class party

503) It takes more words to introduce, express, and adequately elaborate an idea in speech than it takes in writing

504) This makes it necessary for speakers to talk longer about their points

505) using more words on them than would be used to express the same idea in writing.

506) The passage on the difference between writing and **speech** explains why speech takes more **words** to **elaborate** an idea than writing.

507) Still, "there are times you've got to say 'no,'" explains the warranty expert of the company, such as when a product is undamaged or has been abused.

508) When Thorp has tried everything to resolve a complaint and realizes that the customer will be dissatisfied no matter what

509) she returns her attention to the rest of her customers, who she says are "the reason for my success."

510) This passage that **questions** whether the customer is always right emphasizes that sometimes **unreasonable** demand should be **rejected**.

511) Being visually overstimulated, the children have a great deal of difficulty concentrating and end up with worse academic results

512) On the other hand, if there is not much decoration on the classroom walls, the children

are less distracted, spend more time on their activities, and learn more

513) So it's our job, in order to support their attention, to find the right balance between excessive decoration and the complete absence of it

514) **Advocating** a recent study from Carnegie Mellon University, the passage **underscores** the importance of the **adequate** amount of class decoration.

515) Groups can share resources, care for sick members, scare off predators, fight together against enemies, divide tasks so as to improve efficiency, and contribute to survival in many other ways

516) In particular, if an individual and a group want the same resource, the group will generally prevail, so competition for resources would especially favor a need to belong

517) Belongingness will likewise promote reproduction, such as by bringing potential mates into contact with each other, and in particular by keeping parents together to care for their children, who are much more likely to survive if they have more than one caregiver.

518) Dividing main topic with survival and **reproduction**, the passage explains the **usefulness** of belonging for human **evolution**.

519) Those that are brave enough to take those roads less travelled are able to get great returns and derive major satisfaction out of their courageous moves

520) You must learn to take those chances that many people around you will not take

521) because your success will flow from those bold decisions that you will take along the way

522) The passage **encourages** readers to get out of the safe zones and be brave to take **unknown** roads to attain the greatest levels of **potential**.

523) One possible reason is that many thousands of years ago humans lived in a world of dangerous predators where they had to have their wits about them at all times to avoid being killed

524) We are smaller than our ancestors too, and it is a characteristic of domestic animals that they are generally smaller than their wild cousins

525) None of this may mean we are dumber — brain size is not necessarily an indicator of human intelligence — but it may mean that our brains

today are wired up differently, and perhaps more efficiently, than those of our ancestors

526) The passage on the **shrunk** size of human brain tries to find why it has, and **concludes** that changed living **condition** played a huge role.

527) Whatever the case, it is your body that has the intelligence to regain health, and not the herbs

528) Try to imagine how herbs might come into your body and intelligently fix your problems

529) Otherwise, it would mean that herbs are more intelligent than the human body, which is truly hard to believe

530) With the concept of bodily **intelligence**, the passage tries to break **common** misbelief that certain herbs can have **particular** effect on selective organs.

531) grabbing products off shelves and moving them to where they can be packed and dispatched

532) tells them where to go and what to do, controlling the smallest details of their movements

533) Rather than asking us to think or adapt

534) By **introducing** Jennifer, a piece of software, the passage **argues** that robots not only has taken our jobs but also our **judgment**.

535) People are influenced by the physical and social contexts in which they live

536) making one-on-one interactions and creating opportunities for learning

537) By engaging the world around them, thinking, being curious, and interacting with people, objects, and the world around them

538) Putting infant's **development** on the center, the passage on developmental science provides an **insight** that individuals **regardless** of ages can be an active contributor of development.

539) While freshness is now being used as a term

540) has legally allowed institutional waste

541) with freshly made sandwiches

542) Alerting readers of the **environmental** costs behind the demand for freshness, the passage introduces **specific** harms that is involved in the process of **producing** fresh foods.

543) whether we can listen to two people talk at the same time

544) contained a message that the listener had to repeat back (called "shadowing") while the other ear included people speaking

545) found it was impossible for his participants to know whether the message in the other ear was spoken by a man or woman, in English or another language, or was even comprised of real words at all

546) Introducing an **experiment** that has people hear two different messages **simultaneously**, the passage concludes that people cannot process two pieces of information **at the same time**.

547) the most recent technological boost received by the tourism sector is represented by mobile applications

548) empowering tourists with mobile access to services such as hotel reservations, airline ticketing, and recommendations for local attractions generates strong interest and considerable profits

549) **Analyzing** what has happened with the evolution of ICTs, this passage links technological **advancement**, service provision and customer **loyalty.**

550) live in nations that are net exporters of food

551) The reason people are hungry in those countries is that the products produced there can be sold on the world market for more than the local citizens can afford to pay for them

552) many people are too poor to buy it

553) The passage shortly **summarizes** the reason why people still **starve** despite **excessive** food.

554) when they feel they are at their best

555) make it a point to deal with tasks that demand attention at your best time of the day

556) the muse of creativity awakens and is allowed to roam more freely

557) The passage introduces **novel** insight that **creativity** works best in the worst times of each individual.

558) there is increasing evidence that we are more motivated to tune in to our favorite shows and characters

559) The more television we watch, the less likely we are to volunteer our time or to spend time with people in our social networks

560) the more time we make for Friends, the less time we have for friends in real life

561) This passage on the **limitation** of television in terms of **satisfying** our social needs argues that television can **use up** times for making real social networks.

562) We often associate the concept of temperature with how hot or cold an object feels when we touch it

563) if you stand in bare feet with one foot on carpet and the other on a tile floor, the tile feels colder than the carpet even though both are at the same temperature

564) because tile transfers energy by heat at a higher rate than carpet does

565) With an example situation of standing on two different **surfaces** with the same **temperature** with each foot, the passage shows that our body cannot readily **measure** temperature.

566) meant to convince thousands of resistant alumni to make a donation

567) more than twice as effective as the two combined

568) we triggered their awareness that someone was trying to persuade them — and they shielded themselves against it

569) Through an experiment on making donation, the passage concludes that people **shield** themselves when they **detect** the **intention** of persuasion.

570) in which this reversal of attitudes about certain foods has happened to an entire society

571) a portion of the population hates their consumption and associates it with poverty

572) if the consumption of insects as a food luxury is to be promoted, there would be more chances that some individuals who do not present this habit overcome ideas under which they were educated

573) This passage on the social **perception** on the **edibility** of certain food explores the **underlying** psychology behind each attitude to certain foods.

memo

memo